KT-481-012

OFSTED
Inspections

The Early Experience

DISPOSED OF
BY LIBRARY
HOUSE OF LORDS

EDITED BY

JANET OUSTON, PETER EARLEY
AND BRIAN FIDLER

David Fulton Publishers
London

David Fulton Publishers Ltd
2 Barbon Close, London WC1N 3JX

First published in Great Britain by David Fulton Publishers 1996

Note: The right of Janet Ouston, Peter Earley and Brian Fidler to be
identified as the editors of this work has been asserted by them in
accordance with the Copyright, Designs and Patents Act 1988.

Copyright © David Fulton Publishers Ltd

British Library Cataloguing in Publication Data

A catalogue record for this book is available from the British Library

ISBN 1-85346-408-2

All rights reserved. No part of this publication may be reproduced,
stored in a retrieval system or transmitted, in any form, or by any
means, electronic, mechanical, photocopying, recording or otherwise,
without the prior permission of the publishers.

Typeset by Textype Typesetters, Cambridge
Printed in Great Britain by BPC Books and Journals Ltd., Exeter

Contents

Contributors

David Blunkett is Shadow Secretary of State for Education.

Christopher Bowring-Carr taught in England and abroad for a number of years. He was an education officer in an LEA, a HMI for 15 years and is currently an educational consultant.

Nicola Brimblecombe is a researcher at the Oxford Centre for Education Management at Oxford Brookes University engaged in examining teachers' attitudes towards OFSTED inspections. She is co-author of several papers, and is currently studying education management for a higher degree. Her background is in psychology and research methodology.

Vin Davis is a member of Her Majesty's Inspectorate (HMI). He works in the Research and Analysis team of OFSTED and is based at Alexandra House, London.

Carol Donoughue is a former HMI, an OFSTED Registered Inspector and an OFSTED accredited trainer. She has headed the Institute of Education's Office for Inspection for two years. She has trained and directed OFSTED training courses for primary and lay inspectors.

Peter Earley was a researcher at NFER and is now a Senior Lecturer in the Oxford Centre for Education Management at Oxford Brookes University.

Brian Fidler is Senior Lecturer in the Education Management Centre at the University of Reading.

John Fitz is currently engaged in funded research on school inspectorates in England and Wales. Previous policy research has included an investigation of the Assisted Places Scheme and more recently he has co-directed research into Grant Maintained Schools.

Don Foster is the Liberal Democrat education spokesman.

Derek Glover was for 18 years head of Burford School, Oxfordshire. He has subsequently worked with the education management development teams of Leicester, Keele and the Open universities.

David Hustler is Professor of Education at the Manchester Metropolitan University, and directs the research team which has been investigating the role of the Lay Inspector.

Val Klenowski was a Commonwealth Research Trust scholar at the Institute of Education and is now Senior Lecturer at the Hong Kong Institute of Education.

James Learmonth started teaching in London in 1964. All his experience has been in mixed comprehensive schools and he was head of a school in Tower Hamlets from 1975 to 1980. He was then appointed to HMI and worked in the Educational Disadvantage Unit. He became Chief Inspector in Richmond-upon-Thames in 1989 and since 1993 has worked independently as an advisor to schools and LEAs and as a Registered Inspector.

John Lee is Principal Lecturer in Education at the University of the West of England. He is field leader for Professionally Related Subject Studies.

Rosalind Levačić is Senior Lecturer at the Centre for Educational Policy and Management at the Open University. She has written extensively on Local Management of Schools and on financial and resource management in education.

Janet Maw is Senior Lecturer in the Department of Curriculum Studies at the Institute of Education, University of London. She has published in the areas of curriculum and policy analysis, school textbooks, and HMI. Her concern with inspection stems from an interest in the way forms of evaluation impact on the processes of schooling and curriculum development.

Jean Northam was Dean of Teaching Studies at St Mary's University College, Strawberry Hill (a College of the University of Surrey). She is now director of an educational consultancy – Lilyvale Educational Services – in Exeter.

Maureen O'Connor is an educational journalist and author. She was the first editor of the education page in the *Guardian*, and currently writes for the *Observer*, the *Independent* and the *Times Education Supplement*. She is the author of several books for parents and of *Secondary Education* in the Cassell's Education Matters series.

Michael Ormston is Senior Lecturer in the Oxford Centre for Education Management at Oxford Brookes University, and part of their inspection research team. He is co-author of a best-selling book on inspection, and several papers, and regularly runs workshops nationally and internationally on many aspects of education management.

Janet Ouston is Senior Lecturer at the Institute of Education, London, and head of the Management Development Centre.

Sheila Russell was an LEA Senior Education Inspector and is now a Visiting Fellow at Leeds Metropolitan University. She is a Registered Inspector for OFSTED in the primary and secondary phases and Vice-President of the National Association of Educational Inspectors, Advisors and Consultants.

Marian Shaw is Senior Lecturer in the Oxford Centre for Education Management at Oxford Brookes University, and part of their research team. She is co-author of a book on inspection, and a trained OFSTED Inspector. She runs workshops nationally and internationally on many aspects of education management.

Gillian Shephard is Secretary of State for Education and Employment.

Valerie Stone is Senior Lecturer in Education at the Manchester Metropolitan University. She has been involved in the OFSTED/HEFCE inspection process concerning University Departments of Education.

Abbreviations and Acronyms

AERA	American Educational Research Association
AI	Attached or Additional Inspector
ALI	Association of Lay Inspectors
BERA	British Educational Research Association
CASE	Campaign for the Advancement of State Education
CATE	Council for the Accreditation of Teacher Education
CLEA	Council of Local Education Authorities
DES	Department of Education and Science
DFE	Department for Education
DFEE	Department for Education and Employment
EIS	Education Information System (OFSTED's data base)
GCSE	General Certificate of Secondary Education
GEST	Grants for Education Support and Training
GMS	Grant Maintained Status
HMI	Her Majesty's Inspectorate
HMCI	Her Majesty's Chief Inspector
HMSO	Her Majesty's Stationery Office
INSET	In-Service Education for Teachers
IDP	Institutional Development Plan
KS	Key Stage (of National Curriculum)
LEA	Local Education Authority
LMS	Local Management of Schools
NC	National Curriculum
NALIS	National Association of Lay Inspectors
NFER	National Foundation for Educational Research
OFSTED	Office for Standards in Education
PICSI	Pre-Inspection Context and School Indicators Report
RgI	Registered Inspector
RISE	Research and Information into State Education Trust
RSA	Royal Society of Arts
SDP	School Development Plan
SEN	Special Educational Needs
SI	Senior Inspector
SMT	Senior Management Team
TEC	Training and Enterprise Council
TES	Times Educational Supplement
VFM	Value for Money

Introduction

by Janet Ouston, Peter Earley and Brian Fidler

In 1993 a new pattern of school inspections was introduced. These were planned and managed by the Office for Standards in Education (OFSTED) – a new government department. Details of the new inspection programme are given in Chapter 1. This new national programme of inspection attempted to meet both needs for accountability to central government and parents, and to support school development. The extent to which these two aims could be met within one pattern of inspections is a theme which runs through many of the contributions to this book and its partner (Earley, Fidler and Ouston 1996). The balance in the first two and a half years of inspection (from September 1993 to May 1996) seems to be towards accountability as indicated by the emphasis on comparability of inspection practices across schools. The extent to which standardisation is either desirable, or achievable in practice, however, is raised by several contributors to this book.

The book starts with a description of the new inspection programme from the Office for Standards in Education by Vin Davis. In Chapter 2 John Fitz and John Lee explore the relationship between the changing ways of working of Her Majesty's Inspectorate during the 1970s and 1980s and their impact on policy and pedagogy. They then set out the ways in which OFSTED differs from HMI in these areas.

Janet Maw reviews the explicit purposes and implicit consequences of the OFSTED model of inspection, drawing to our attention the powerful influence of the OFSTED model over school practice. As Power (1995) says in relation to commercial audit 'Concepts of performance and quality are in danger of being defined largely in terms of conformity to the audit process' (p48).

Chapters 4 to 9 are concerned with the inspectors' perspective on inspection. In Chapter 4 Carol Donoughue looks at the training of inspectors and in Chapters 5 and 6, two former HMIs (Christopher Bowring-Carr and James Learmonth) reflect on the expectations and requirements of OFSTED. Can they ever be met within the existing framework? Can inspectors' judgements be valid and reliable? Will they contribute to a process of school development? Do the expectations assume an over-simplified and rational model of a school that denies the reality of school life?

In Chapter 7 David Hustler and Valerie Stone explore this question through their research on Lay Inspectors. What is the purpose of having a Lay Inspector? After how many inspections do they cease to be 'Lay'? How does the Registered Inspector strike a balance between OFSTED's requirement to have a non-educationalist's perspective included in the inspection team, and his or her own requirement to have experienced team members? Ros Levačić and Derek Glover examine inspectors' use of terms such as efficiency, effectiveness and value for money in Chapter 8. They conclude that the use of the terms is far from clear. It may be that schools are too complex organisations with too many diverse outcomes for these terms to be entirely transferable from the commercial context. Jean Northam's analysis of OFSTED reports in Chapter 9 sets out very clearly the inspectors' perceptions of 'a good school' but on the whole these are concerned with the 'whats' of classroom practice rather than the 'hows'.

Chapters 10 to 12 – by Sheila Russell, the editors, and Nicola Brimblecombe and colleagues – focus on the impact of inspection on the school and its governors and parents. The OFSTED logo is 'Improvement through Inspection' and it is in these chapters that we can assess whether this is likely to happen. Do schools' experience of OFSTED seem likely to support, or discourage schools from improving themselves? Chapters 10, 11 and 12 look at schools' responses to inspection and present a mixed picture. Some teachers (and schools) are distressed by the inspection experience , and it may take some time for professional confidence to return. Others report that the experience did assist with school development. But it should be kept in mind that the research seems to show that less experienced teachers, and women, respond more negatively than the more experienced. In addition, our own work was undertaken three months after the inspection when hopefully most schools will be over the worst of the 'post-inspection blues'. Chapters 13 and 14 by Janet Ouston and Val Klenowski, and Maureen O'Connor, report that parents and governors on the whole welcomed their new role in inspection. Many of their concerns overlapped and they made worthwhile suggestions for improving the inspection process.

The book ends with a political perspective with brief contributions from Gillian Shephard, David Blunkett and Don Foster on the future of inspection.

Many of the papers included in this book are updated and extended versions of papers given at a Seminar on Inspection at the British Educational Research Association Conference held in Oxford in September 1994, and convened by Brian Fidler. The book was completed in August 1995, as a new inspection *Framework* is being prepared. This will be implemented in the Summer Term of 1996. OFSTED's *Update Number 15* says that the revision aims to:

make inspection more manageable by inspectors;
make inspection more acceptable and useful to schools;
contribute more effectively to school's strategies for sustained improvement;
result in better evaluation and reporting. (p1)

and continues:

The introduction of the new *Framework* should mean that less work will be required of schools in completing documentation. Greater account will be taken of the school objectives and evidence of its achievements over a period of time. The process of inspection, particularly in primary and special schools will be more sensitive to the demands on teachers and the way the curriculum is planned. Governors and schools will have greater ownership of inspection. In reporting inspection findings there will be a greater focus on the strengths as well as the weaknesses of the school, highlighting the attainment and progress of the school and the quality of teaching. There should be greater clarity of writing with illustration of judgements. Inspection reports will take account of trends in the school's standards, and the school's own strategies for improvement in identifying priority issues for development. (pp2 3)

This new pattern of inspection looks as if it will be more 'school-friendly' and that it may, as a consequence, lead to the balance between accountability and development moving away from accountability and towards development. We look forward to further research on the new OFSTED *Framework*.

Part One: OFSTED Inspections

CHAPTER ONE

The Early Experience of OFSTED

by Vin Davis

In this review of the Office for Standards in Education's (OFSTED) first two years it seemed appropriate that OFSTED should itself have an opportunity to put the new inspection system in context. The first years of the new system have seen a rise in OFSTED's critical profile and, hopefully, a growth in public understanding of its functions and activities. This chapter looks in detail at OFSTED's role in the inspection process and examines the ways in which it has sought to improve the system.

The Office for Standards in Education was established as a new government department in September 1992; its general purpose was to improve standards of achievement and quality of education through regular independent inspection, public reporting and informed advice to ministers. OFSTED took over responsibility for monitoring inspection of schools from the LEAs. Until then LEA inspections had tended to be variable in coverage, both over time and geographically, and the absence of national benchmarking resulted in some inconsistency. Responsibility for the four-year inspection cycle lies with the Secretary of State; OFSTED's role is to regulate and manage an efficient school inspection system and to plan for its future. Part of its brief was that all schools in England should be inspected within four years.

Under the new system, OFSTED does not employ its inspectors, but contracts them by tender. Inspectors are required to make judgements on four main areas:

- the quality of education provided;
- the quality of standards achieved;
- the efficient management of the school's financial arrangements;

- the spiritual, moral and cultural development of pupils.

In setting up the system, OFSTED had the following imperatives in mind:

- the importance of national consistency;
- the importance of supporting schools' action and development planning;
- the importance of judging standards and quality at all levels of teaching and learning.

It was for this reason that a common *Framework* (OFSTED 1994b) was established by statute and supported by a *Handbook for Inspection* (OFSTED 1994a). The *Framework* provides a clear and comprehensive set of criteria which is intended to establish the optimum in consistency and objectivity. The focus of inspection is the child in the classroom; the *Framework* enables inspectors to look at standards of provision, standards of pupil achievement and other contributory factors in any type of school with this in mind.

Some critics of the OFSTED inspection model argue that an identical set of observations and a common *Framework* cannot guarantee that inspectors will always be able to agree on the quality of a lesson. However, benchmarking, training, monitoring, regular updating of the *Framework*, and regular changes in inspection teams all help to promote consistency; they also ensure that there are more checks on the validity and reliability of judgements under the new system than at any time in England's 150 year history of statutory school inspection.

OFSTED is concerned to ensure that inspection processes are consistent, reliable and intelligible. But in the drive towards these goals it is important that the less measurable or more creative aspects of education are not unwittingly filtered out. As Her Majesty's Chief Inspector (HMCI) stated in his Annual Report (OFSTED 1995a), 'if inspection is perceived as imposing uniformity, discouraging initiative or stifling imagination, its capacity to bring about improvement will be undermined.'

An OFSTED inspection report offers the school an analysis of what is working and what is not working; it is the school's report, for the school to use in whatever way it sees fit. Post-inspection action may be required, but the form of that action is not prescribed. It is the responsibility of the head teacher and governing body to act on the recommendations of the report, with the help of the LEA if appropriate. It is not part of OFSTED's responsibility to provide post-inspection support.

Some schools find it challenging to improve themselves – they need support from a variety of external sources. It is not uncommon for

OFSTED to be told that improvement through inspection will not work unless inspection is accompanied by advice, that inspectors need to engage in discussion with teachers; but the regulations which govern inspection do not require inspectors to give advice or to justify their judgements to schools. It is for the school to decide how it might best act upon inspection findings, drawing on the expertise of others where appropriate.

The inspection system produces a very great deal of information about education in England. Around 1,000 inspections in 1993/94 and 6,000 each year in the future provide a valuable resource enabling national characteristics to be established and schools to be compared like with like. OFSTED has designed a central database system – the Education Information System (EIS) – to collate the output from these inspections. The database has two components:

- the text of all inspection reports, records of inspection evidence, subject summary forms, lesson observation forms, and supplementary evidence forms;
- numerical and other coded data, including subject information, the head teacher's form, and judgement assessments.

Data from other sources, such as the annual DFEE Form 7 school census and the public examination performance tables, is collated with EIS data.

Reports from inspections provide a 'snapshot' view of a large sample of schools, but they cannot provide all the detailed evidence necessary for HMCI to give advice on particular issues. Data from inspections are therefore supplemented by evidence from more specifically focused inspection of schools by Her Majesty's Inspectors of Schools (HMI); taken together the two sources of information put OFSTED in a strong position to comment on the quality of education provided in schools and to suggest ways of improving it.

Under the Education (Schools) Act 1992, HMCI also has a duty to review the standards of independent inspections and reports made by registered inspectors (RgIs). In order to fulfil this duty, HMCI arranged for inspections to be monitored by HMI, the professional staff of OFSTED. During the first year of independent inspections of secondary schools, HMI monitoring has taken two forms: visits to schools to observe the conduct of inspections, and checks on inspection reports. Follow-up inspections of some of the schools are also an important part of this process. HMI assessment of RgI inspections helps to throw light on the strengths of inspection practice and to suggest areas for further development for individual RgIs and for the whole system.

It is too soon to know whether the OFSTED inspection system is successful. Monitoring at many levels suggests that, overall, the new system has made a promising start. Any flaws are understandable given the difficulty of establishing, in a short period of time, an inspection system based on independent RgIs all working to a common set of criteria and procedures. The way in which RgIs have conducted their inspections has generally been of a high standard. However, some inspection reports do not provide such clear and informative evaluation and are less well written; good grammar is less important than clear and informative evaluation. OFSTED has given priority to following up RgIs who demonstrate serious weaknesses in their management of an inspection or in the writing of their report. However, statistics on RgIs monitored more than once show that 78 per cent have either maintained high standards of inspection or improved on their earlier performance.

RgIs are drawing on their early experiences to improve inspections and act on HMI comments on their performance. No one should underestimate the challenge presented by introducing a national system of independent inspection on this scale. Neither OFSTED nor the independent inspectors would claim that the system is perfect, but the experience of the early years has shown what can be achieved and already areas for further improvement have been identified (for example, the clarity and precision of evaluation in written reports).

In his report (OFSTED 1995a) on the quality and service of inspection 1993/94, HMCI reviewed the work of OFSTED in regulating and managing the new school inspection system and planning for the future. He concluded that the year 1993/94 may well prove to have been a turning-point in the implementation of the Government's educational reforms. Education is now recognised as too important and too expensive a public service for schools not to be accountable to the local communities they serve.

In its second year of existence OFSTED has concentrated on issues of quality and service and on trying to meet its inspection targets. A number of initiatives have been introduced to make the inspection system in OFSTED and in schools more effective by:

- providing high quality advice at the national education level to inform policy development and evaluate the effects of policy;
- examining ways in which the inspection process can support particular schools in their work;
- focusing inspection on the individual class or lesson, the critical area for achieving significant change.

The achievement of a four-year cycle of school inspection, a major part of OFSTED's remit, was strongly reaffirmed by the Secretary of State in her North of England speech this year. To this end, OFSTED launched its Additional Inspector (AI) initiative to overcome the shortfall in the inspection cycle of primary and special schools by appointing suitably qualified individuals as AIs in OFSTED's primary and secondary school inspection programme. After training and induction, in which they will work alongside HMIs, AIs will take part in and lead inspection teams. AI posts, offered either as a fixed term contract or as a secondment normally lasting for a year, are considered to be particularly suitable for head teachers and deputy head teachers and will provide valued professional development opportunities.

In the coming year, OFSTED intends to carry out a review of its second round of inspection and revise its inspection strategies accordingly. Any such revision would be designed to:

- make inspection more manageable for inspectors;
- make inspection more acceptable and useful to schools;
- contribute more effectively to schools' strategies for sustained improvement;
- improve evaluation and reporting.

OFSTED is also looking at ways of reducing the bureaucracy of inspection. The overall aim is to ensure that inspection will, in future, provide clear and unequivocal evaluation for parents and for the school without being burdensome and stressful for all involved, especially for teachers and inspectors. A new *Framework for Inspection* has been developed after wide consultation and, to support the *Framework*, a new *Handbook* in three versions, for primary, secondary and special school inspections, will provide phase-specific guidance. Inspection reports will also take greater account of trends in, and the school's own strategies for, improvement.

Another important aspect of OFSTED's work is the production of inspection 'tools' to assist RgIs in undertaking their work. The most important tool for this purpose is the Pre-Inspection Context and School Indicator (PICSI) report. PICSIs have been continually updated and improved since they were first introduced. Currently, the results of the research published as *Assessing School Effectiveness* (OFSTED 1994c) are being incorporated into the PICSI.

OFSTED is also continuing to develop its research and development programme. The EIS database now contains very extensive information. It is being increasingly used to throw light on key questions of educational effectiveness and efficiency, such as the links between class size and quality of teaching, and between resources and outputs. Most of this work is being undertaken by OFSTED itself, but use of the EIS database by outside researchers is also being established.

OFSTED has also decided to embark on a series of research reviews, five of which were commissioned from external researchers in 1994/95, on maths teaching, achievement by minority ethnic pupils, effective learning styles and strategies, international comparisons, and school effectiveness research. A good deal of educational research is written for other researchers and fails to inform and guide the decisions of practising teachers; the aim of the OFSTED reviews is to put research findings directly into the hands of teachers.

Increased inspection activity has placed greater emphasis on research directly related to inspection issues. Thus there is scope for research into the impact of inspection on school improvement. OFSTED is co-operating with members of the research community in developing and testing a range of theories of school inspection which we intend to feed back into thinking on the best design for inspection and the criteria which are applied during inspection.

Looking forward, OFSTED is likely to continue to commission a number of reviews of research in key areas. Among the research projects likely to be developed are work on education of particular groups of pupils, such as those who are gifted or particularly able, a reading survey in collaboration with three LEAs, and an investigation of standards over time in public examinations, as well as work that draws on the EIS data-base. In April 1995 OFSTED made inspection reports available on Internet; over 1,500 reports are now available to users throughout the world. Our immediate aim is for the reports to be more readily accessible to the general public.

In conclusion, inspection offers a fresh and independent view and, hopefully, helpful recommendations for development. It identifies both strengths and weaknesses which, when viewed positively, may be used by the school to bring about desired change. Parental involvement is crucial in this process; parents are a key client group. It is important to remember that OFSTED inspection is a *Parent Charter* initiative. Inspection should be a joint venture, requiring positive attitudes from all involved. In looking to the future, OFSTED wishes to encourage schools to depart from their current practice of somewhat sterile policy writing (brought on, no doubt, by *Framework* requirements, now amended) to that of policy linked to self-review. There needs to be a shift in emphasis away from policy writing towards self-review. If self-review can be seen as an unthreatening norm, then periodic external review reinforces and adds an extra perspective to school self-evaluation, providing a focus for improvement and a catalyst for change.

Part Two: The Handbook

CHAPTER TWO

Where angels fear ...

by John Fitz and John Lee

Introduction

The Education (Schools) Act 1992 significantly transformed the mode of school inspection. It replaced Her Majesty's Inspectorate (HMI), a small body of professionally independent inspectors, established in 1839, with HMCI/OFSTED. The responsibility for school inspections was thus assumed by privatised inspection teams contracted from the centre, guided by a framework document and overseen by a small number of HMIs. In this chapter we trace some of the evident similarities and differences between the two modalities of inspection but with a particular focus on the Inspectorate's continuing involvement in the development and regulation of educational change.

We have previously argued that regardless of their public statements HMI were involved in the making of policy and in particular took a real interest in pedagogy (Fitz and Lee 1994). What we stated then was that in our view 'It is difficult to see how the annual report from Her Majesty's Chief Inspector can have the same impact as recent annual reports of the previous Chief Inspector' (but) 'It may well be that because of the way that OFSTED focuses on the system rather than on policy-makers and politicians, it will have a more rapid and profound effect on pedagogy.' The recent report of Chris Woodhead, HMCI, in his RSA lecture, and Jim Rose (Director of Inspection) tend to support this contention (*TES*, 10 March 1995).

This chapter examines some of the ways in which changes in the inspection of schools, changes in personnel and the historic legitimacy of

HMI contribute to both the legitimacy and authority of HMCI/OFSTED statements. In doing this we first turn to HMI as it existed up to 1992.

Her Majesty's Inspectorate – a brief history

Constitutionally the role of HMI was to provide the government of the day with a description of the 'health' of the system. They did not formally have the brief to create policy although they were expected to advise and occasionally comment on both policy proposals and the consequences of policy change. This central role hardly impacted on the daily life of the vast majority of inspectors. They were appointed to and operated in particular geographic areas. Leonard Clark's reminiscences provide an interesting if uncritical picture of the work of an inspector up to the early 1960s (Clark 1976). Basically the inspectors 'job' was to know the schools on her or his 'patch', to visit them and to write reports. The reports were confidential but provided evidence of the state of a particular school to its head, the LEA and the Chief Inspector. We have had this description of HMI work confirmed in an interview with a retired inspector who served throughout the period of the 60s, 70s and early 80s. HMI's role in the maintenance and improvement of quality and standards related directly to the inspection reports' comments on the institution visited and the use of those reports as feedback on the health of the system. What we draw from reading HMI documents of the period, published reminiscences and interviews is that the Inspectorate neither saw itself, nor was seen, as a powerful actor in policy making fora.

The period following the implementation of the 1944 Act was clearly one of change and we argue that individual HMIs played a part in that change. The work of two inspectors, Christian Schiller and John Blackie, shows individual inspectors embarking on a struggle over pedagogy. What these two, and other similarly 'charismatic' members of the Inspectorate sought to do was to establish a model of good practice in primary schools and offer that model to selected teachers. These HMIs had a view of what constituted quality in primary education This good practice did not have explicit pedagogic principles; rather, it drew its inspiration from the Romantic movement, from Rousseau, Montessori and to some degree from the psychology of Jean Piaget. If it had actual antecedents it was in some of the private schools established by and for middle class intellectuals in the 1930s, such as Dartford School and The Maltings. What we are saying here is that reform was pragmatic: these inspectors sought to change the work of individual teachers and schools, not create national educational policy. It is notable that those teachers who were presented as models and those to whom the models were presented were specially selected.

The creation of the Schools Council in 1962 provided HMI with a direct entry into curriculum reform. All the curriculum groups established had HMI members and many of these were extremely influential in their own right. Edith Biggs, for instance, was responsible for the first Schools Council publication and established through that a particular vision of the content and teaching method of primary mathematics, effectively defining what were the markers of quality provision in school mathematics. That HMIs as individuals can be seen to be influential in the whole range of curriculum areas is easy to substantiate but what cannot be substantiated is a central agenda setting and policy drive.

A new set up

In the late 1960s, however, the historic functions of HMI came under the critical scrutiny of a parliamentary Select Committee. Its Report in 1968 recommended that the Secretary of State's 'duty' to cause inspections be replaced by a 'power' to initiate inspections as and when necessary; full and formal inspections should cease except in exceptional circumstances and that LEA advisory inspections services should undertake the bulk of inspections (DES 1982, p8). This may well have marked the low point of HMI's influence on both central policy making and on school practice.

Indeed, one of our informants, a very long-serving inspector, stated: 'nobody, not even some of my colleagues, could remember the Chief Inspector before Sheila Browne'. A point confirmed by Eric Bolton, who stated that the continued existence of HMI was in serious doubt in the 1970s:

> 'HMI came perilously close to disappearing at that stage because they were like that film, like forgotten to death.' (Senior Chief Inspector interview)

What Browne did is very significant. She made crucial organisational changes to the Inspectorate and set an agenda for action for the service as a whole. The organisational changes were very significant in that by creating a powerful centre group she was creating what might be called a policy task group and locating them next to powerful civil servants. This group were able to draw on data collected by their territorial colleagues and were involved in the newer style of national initiatives established by Browne. Browne, according to Bolton, was clear that while politicians and the DES were concerned largely with the issues of teacher supply and reform of the secondary system, it was open to HMI to establish a policy agenda themselves. HMI should be concerned with curriculum, quality and standards, policy issues that Browne saw as becoming significant in ten years' time. What HMI engaged in was the creation of two major surveys. *Primary Education in England: A Survey by HMI* (DES 1978) and *Aspects of Secondary Education: A Survey by HMI* (DES 1979) became very important documents in the Inspectorate's policy initiatives. One of our informants – a retired Senior Inspector – stressed their empirical validity:

> 'What struck me as a young HMI was that virtually every sentence that there is there, has behind it several pages of data, every evaluative statement is firmly rooted ...'

A colleague of his with a similar length of service but spent as a territorial inspector agreed and underlined the significance of the *Survey* in policy making:

> '... HMI were key because they had the up to date evidence from visits to schools and the Secondary Survey ... which was published in 1979 but really took place from 1975 gave incontrovertible evidence of the need really for much more steering of a curriculum for secondary schools.'

In brief, the Browne reorganisation not merely created a policy group but, as important, directed HMI visits to gather data relevant to the policy making agenda she had set. The two surveys referred to above are actually the first of a series of such national sampling and reflection on the system. The *Rayner Report* quotes The Assistant Masters and Mistresses' Association, saying that the two national surveys and other documents 'have been a very significant contribution by the Inspectorate to the debates on matters of vital importance.' (DES 1982, p14).

An interpretive community

It is clear from our informants and from the evidence gathered by the *Rayner Report* (1982) that HMI's judgements and comments were highly respected by the profession and by policy makers, at least until the Thatcher era (DES 1982, pp13–4). Moreover, that report had the medium term effect of consolidating HMI as an authoritative source of information relating to the workings and effectiveness of the education system. The legitimacy of their judgements and opinions also derived from their particular mode of operation and the close knit nature of the HMI community. Stanley Fish (1980, 1989) argues that the authority and legitimacy of literary critics resides in the fact they constitute an 'interpretive community'. He argues that such a community has authority from its institutional position, a shared enterprise and most importantly that they are both the producers and reproducers of knowledge. The concept of an interpretive community does not require consensus or agreement among its practitioners; Fish's point is that regardless of violent disagreement, literary critics and literary criticism still have authority and legitimacy.

Our interviewees all stressed the individuality of their colleagues and the way in which internally HMI took radically different opinions. The following from a Senior Inspector is typical:

'... I felt that HMI was very – now this is a very personal view of it – HMI was a group of individuals who, and it was often said too, that when ten HMIs were gathered together there were eleven opinions and I think it was the eleventh opinion which was the strength, *the collective judgement of HMI* [our emphasis] ...'.

The induction of new recruits is significant and we have evidence from our interview data that from the 1970s it became much more systematic. Clarke's account of his induction as an assistant inspector, is very much a story of his apprenticeship in a particular locality, his duty being to report to his inspector, not the centre. Another informant gives a clear picture of induction as apprenticeship in the 1960s: 'you learned the ropes from established colleagues learnt on the job, all that stuff from London seemed much less important then.'

This aspect of induction, learning alongside future colleagues never lost its importance; according to our informants it was particularly valued.

'... I was mentored from the 'Borchester' office by a scientist, we would not be mentored by people of our own subject and I was mentored by a scientist and enjoyed that aspect and learnt a great deal, I mean my learning curve became almost vertical.' (Senior Inspector, 1970s entrant)

The need to ensure all inspectors were given a similar training is spelled out by Eric Bolton:

This component (of induction and training) is divided into: introduction to aspects of the system with which the new HMI, because of their own specialisms, are so far unfamiliar; and introduction to issues of current concern and new developments in the system. The first must be an individualised programme and new HMIs make visits with appropriate specialists which introduce them to new phases or institutions – for example, an FHE engineering specialist may visit nursery classes and youth centres. The second is achieved largely though centrally and locally organised seminars and through participation in general courses. (Bolton, in Hopes 1991)

The position of HMI with regard to policy is described as an 'interface' and the relation of inspection to policy making and the need for HMIs to know the mechanisms of policy making are made clear by the Senior Chief Inspector:

Through national courses and through short attachments to *senior colleagues* [our emphasis], new HMIs learn of HMIs relationship with officials and

Ministers, tracing the routes through which policy advice, *based on inspection* (our emphasis), is made available. (Bolton, in Hopes 1991)

On entry new HMIs had to go on:

'... the new boys' course in London and there you spent some time with civil servants learning about the departments, officials' work and so on and you met some senior members of the Inspectorate. I remember being in a seminar where Sheila Browne was present and Bill Pile was present who was the permanent secretary to the department at that time, Shirley Williams was the minister, she wasn't there, but they were talking about how the department might delve into what was becoming widely known as the secret garden of the curriculum.' (Interview, Senior Inspector)

Effectively HMI created themselves as a small cohesive body able through their own training and procedures to accept and interpret each others' judgements. The often repeated phrases 'pressure of experience' and 'collective judgement' arise from this as we illustrate above. What we have here is the way in which HMIs are trained to become producers of knowledge.

We must now turn to the reproduction of knowledge. Inspectors in the field gathered data from both inspections of schools and more informal visits. All of this data was recorded. The smaller group of HMIs at the centre were able to reproduce this knowledge to support and argue for policies. One of our informants made specific reference to this process.

'We were as HMIs the sounding board for many of the 'Office's' ideas that they had, ideas about how they wanted to progress and we had real ideas about the patch. We had street 'cred', we were very credible because we were actually out there and we could tell them what it was really like and what impact their thinking would have upon the patch. It was our job to say how it was rather than how it should be but we did often talk to the 'Office' off the record about the impact of certain things.'

The same informant also speaks of the 'Office' 'backing off' indicating how HMI saw their data being used centrally. The three reports of the Chief Inspector (DES 1989b, 1990, 1991b) use data collected by the Inspectorate, summarise and in doing so offer both a critique of government policy and a direction in which the system ought to go in order to maintain quality and improve standards. The increasing importance of HMI at the centre, in the field of policy making is noted also in the *Rayner Report*, where it is recorded:

Some to whom we have spoken ... have suggested that the role of HM Inspectorate, despite some changes in the late 1960s, has lately become increasingly dominated by its functions in relation to central government. DES 1982, p8)

Policy creation

Where HMI have undoubtedly had a major policy impact is in the development of a national curriculum. That is not only the view of our interviewees but is also a view expressed in the *Rayner Report*. Even in 1982 it records:

> But it is clear that there would be no national emerging policy for the curriculum without the work of HM Inspectorate. There is a clear and unmistakable link between the judgements contained in HM Inspectorate's surveys of primary and secondary education and the views on the curriculum enunciated by the government in its document *The School Curriculum*. (DES 1982, p41)

The documents produced by HMI after the two surveys clearly created a professional climate which enabled the National Curriculum to be written. *The Secondary Survey* (DES 1979) specifically pointed to the problem of variability of curriculum provision between schools and variability of curriculum provision within schools. The *Primary Survey* (DES 1978) also indicated a concern that the curriculum lacked breadth but laid greater stress on the need to 'match' the needs of individual pupils. Although both surveys note that the majority of provision may be described as satisfactory, a significant minority of provision is seen as lacking quality. The *Curriculum Matters* series which followed in the wake of the two surveys set out in an outline manner a 'national curriculum'. Once the 1988 Bill became law and the subject groups had been set up, HMI still played a role in the making of the documents but the differences between the documents and their specificity, in contrast to *Curriculum Matters*, indicates that HMI rather lost the struggle for the curriculum. One of our interviewees noted that:

> 'Instead of thinking collectively about aspects of the curriculum they were suddenly appointed the task of being assessors and observers on subject committees and didn't play the creative and formative role they were used to playing when they were.' (Senior Inspector interview)

He goes on to say '... the ones I knew felt that they had become in a way eunuchs in the system'.

What we can see here is a struggle for the detail of the curriculum. Our contention that HMI were the central policy actors in the creation of the curriculum can be substantiated at the level of establishing a climate and pushing professional policy makers into agreement. What our informant is commenting on is how in the politically charged field of detailed policy creation, the power of HMI, and their legitimacy as an interpretive community was challenged by crude party politics. The assertion by the 'new right' of the ideological problem posed by established institutions whose members could not be guaranteed to be 'one of us' challenged the legitimacy of HMI in an entirely novel manner. The power of an interpretive community was challenged and undermined by critics who refused to accept that HMI judgements were grounded in experience and reflected collective professional wisdom. It was precisely this professionalism that was deemed to be ideological and as a result HMI were not a body to be trusted either as policy makers/advisors, nor even as proper judges of quality.

The Inspectorate's concern for quality and standards could not be addressed through curriculum reform alone. The National Curriculum goes some way to decreasing variability and ensuring entitlement. What this policy did not answer was the 'problem' of one in four lessons being inadequate. This problem in policy terms can only be effected by addressing pedagogy.

Pedagogy

The 'traditional' HMI stance on pedagogy, as noted in the opening of this chapter, was that of expressing judgement on practice as 'good of its kind'. HMI explanations of their work, both published and from interviews, reiterates a neutral stance to pedagogy.

'One of the messages that has always been strong in HMI training has been not to espouse a particular kind of practice. I can remember that being said to me very firmly in my training year and you'll find people are still saying that: that we're concerned with standards and not with particular pedagogy and we're not here to commend specific practice.' (Senior HMI interview)

An ex-colleague of his made the same point:

'Individuals were not there to push particular pedagogic lines, in the schools that they visited the first question that must be in mind was what are you as a school trying to do and the judgement then resulted from some assessment of what the school's own intentions and aims were ...'. (Senior HMI interview)

This was official HMI policy. When they eventually published documents in the 1980s, that point was made very explicit. It does however sit uneasily with HMI action in the late 1960s and 1970s when many inspectors were involved in Schools Council Projects, or through the mechanism of short courses, proposed particular 'visions' of education. This ambiguous stance to pedagogy reflects a coyness over the question of pedagogy, a typically English 'pragmatism'. Brian Simon makes the point rather better in commenting on the work of the Schools Council:

But the key feature of this effort (educational change) has been the atheoretical, pragmatic approach adopted (together with the implicit acceptance of the status quo in organizational and administrative terms) ....

The overall approach can hardly be called systematic, and certainly has not been informed by any generally accepted (or publicly formulated) ideas or theories about the nature of the child or the learning/teaching process – by any 'science of teaching' or pedagogy. (Simon 1985, p78)

Simon goes on to note that no psychological underpinning for the Schools Council programmes was provided and this accounts for the lack of enthusiasm in schools for them. HMI, as we stated earlier, were deeply involved in the work of the Schools Council and were party to the pragmatism to which Simon refers. Davies notes that even in the *British Journal of In-service Education* there is a refusal to discuss pedagogy:

We talk about everything else ad lib., we are content experts, assessment experts, grouping experts, and structure experts. But when it comes to 'teaching methods' and their meaning, we lapse into silence, confusion or at best, a vision somewhere fixed at the end of our noses. (Davies 1994)

However, in the Primary Survey (DES 1978) we see emerge at last the inkling of a pedagogical concept, the idea of 'match'. 'Match' – a term that has become very significant in HMI vocabulary is, however, a rather loose and ill-defined concept. It is employed to refer to the match between curriculum content and the class or group as well as to refer to 'matching' the needs of individuals. It is the latter use that comes closer to Simon's demand for psychological principles to theorise practice. It is possible to identify some of the features that HMI began to use to identify good practice during the 1980s (Lee and Fitz 1994):

1. Curriculum breadth is desirable but it is of equal importance that it is common to all, thus overcoming the problem of variability. Match here means teachers must clearly define knowledge and employ appropriate instructional devices.

2. The curriculum can only be effectively delivered by teachers with a profound knowledge of their subject area and the phase-related needs of learners. What is implied here is that effective pedagogy is at least in part characterised by strong 'classification' and 'framing'.

3. Good practice is identified by meeting the needs of individual pupils, by careful differentiation.

The clearest expression of these principles is to be seen in the CATE criteria set out in Circular 24/89 (DES 1989a).

We are not arguing that HMI had a fully worked out pedagogy but that they were pursuing through their published work, inspection reports and advice to politicians a pedagogical line. In doing this they were both producers of particular discourses and were appropriating others (Bernstein 1993). HMI had been, and continue to be, subject to severe strictures from the 'new right' as the major proponents of progressivism. The reiteration by HMI that they were only concerned to judge what they saw in its own terms, to say that it was 'good of its kind', clearly left them with no policy position. Their strong support for a curriculum in which subjects were explicit and learning clearly related to age and phase in effect seized part of the discourses advanced by the 'new right' and ideologically transformed them from the political to the professional. A generalised but still recognisable pedagogy was advanced and has become the accepted and perhaps acceptable discourse. These are bold claims but HMI's concerns for differentiation and their desire that 'children become effective autonomous learners' (Interview, Senior HMI) show them also struggling for pupil identity. Differentiation and entitlement are also indicative for the struggle in Davies' words over 'who is entitled to what and how that entitlement is delivered' (Davies 1994).

OFSTED

The production of the 'three wise men' report (Alexander, Rose and Woodhead 1992) marks, in a way, a change to a more public expression of a national policy directing pedagogy. Drawing on both academic research and evidence from HMI inspection the report argued that primary school teachers were in the 'grip of dogma' and that this ideological adherence to certain pedagogies resulted in poor teaching in some 25 per cent of Key Stage 2 classes. The OFSTED paper *Primary Matters* (OFSTED 1994d) reiterated the same point as does the follow-up study to the 1991 report. These documents form a crucial bridge between HMI and OFSTED/HMCI. The first, produced before the 1992 Act, led to changes in inspection procedures and personnel. The Act draws on the accumulated evidence, the 'pressure of experience' of HMI and their reports. It is this as much as its particular review of academic research that provides its legitimacy.

Jim Rose, Director of Inspection at OFSTED, claims that the focus of policy should now be on pedagogy and that this concern stems from:

> Inspection findings drawn from a greater number of lesson observations than has been available to HMI, including more full inspections of primary schools by HMI in the course of a year than ever before. The picture of standards which emerges from inspections over the 1993–94 school year is all too familiar. HMI have been reporting that around 30% of lessons are unsatisfactory or poor since our annual reports began in the late 1980s. (Rose 1995, p19)

The explicit appeal to HMI seeks to create a continuity of discourse between the old and new inspection patterns. Although the claim that a greater number of inspections have been conducted is obviously true the security of these judgements is arguably more tenuous. What is conflated here is authority of interpretation, in Fish's terms, and the size of the data set. This is apparent when we remember that the debate about pedagogy, particularly at Key Stage 2, has its roots in HMI concerns about curriculum match and quality. As we have argued above, HMI established at least a climate in which a push for subject specialist teaching, and less use of group discovery work, could begin. It is from this that OFSTED draws some legitimacy. Rose goes on to say this:

> What was it about the teaching of those 'below the line lessons' (ie the 30% identified as being unsatisfactory) that stood in the way of pupils making better progress and reaching higher standards.... First, in some lessons the pupils received very little direct teaching.... Second, the assessment of the pupils' capabilities left much to be desired.... Third, the teachers' subject knowledge was not sufficient to match the developing abilities of the pupils. (Rose 1995)

Rose's article is in part an explication, in part a defence of HMCI Woodhead's 1995 Annual Lecture. In contrast to HMI's previous disavowal of any pursuit of a policy on pedagogy and presumably against his own training as an HMI, Rose now argues that not merely should a debate about pedagogy be engaged in but that the parameters of that debate are already set. Woodhead is more direct than this, laying out in some detail over what the engagement will be about. He confidently asserts, with no recourse to evidence, that:

> What, too often, we have is an emotional commitment to beliefs about the purposes and conduct of education which militates against any genuinely searching educational debate. A commitment, for example, to the belief that education must be relevant to the immediate needs and interests of children; that the teaching of knowledge must be less important than the development of core skills; that the adjective 'didactic' must necessarily have pejorative connotations. (Woodhead 1995, p4)

Although Woodhead claims that what is required is a professional culture which is 'more open minded, more sceptical of the received wisdom, more flexible and probing, less eager to take refuge in simplistic and untenable dichotomies' his reliance upon Oakeshott and his simplistic belief in direct cultural transmission rather belies this. The problem of Woodhead's rhetoric and the conflation of HMI experience and OFSTED procedures is succinctly commented on by Colin White, the Honorary Secretary for former HMI (Schools). In his letter responding to Woodhead's lecture he challenges over five points:

> First, where is the evidence to justify dismissing the collective wisdom of many experts on teaching methods he so readily despises? Second, what enables Christopher Woodhead to ignore the failures and imperfections of 'traditional' teaching methods? Third, is it not possible that variations of both

methods have a place in good teaching? Fourth, why is it now rare for an inspection of a school to be followed up with appropriate advice? Fifth, is it right for the head of our educational inspectorate to express apparently unsubstantiated opinions on such matters? (White 1995, p21)

White might have quoted from the *Annual Report of Her Majesty's Chief Inspector of Schools* (OFSTED 1995a). 'The primary school sample consisted almost entirely of medium to large-sized schools covering Key Stages 1 and 2; the findings of these inspections *may be unrepresentative of the phase as a whole* (our emphasis).'

The number of publications that OFSTED/HMCI have published is quite remarkable. For instance, the end of inspection year 1993/94 has seen the publication of the *Annual Report of the Chief Inspector* and separate reports on the ten subjects of the National Curriculum and on Information Technology and Religious Education. Even more remarkable is the certainty of judgements offered. On the basis of inspection evidence '... from inspections of 79 primary schools by Her Majesty's Inspectors of Schools (HMI) to train Registered Inspectors (RgIs)' and the fact that '... in most of the primary schools ... mathematics was inspected by trainee RgIs ...', OFSTED states 'There are concerns about *standards of achievement in relation to pupils' capabilities* in about a third of primary schools' (OFSTED 1995a). It is then confidently stated that the pedagogical problem is one of '... **challenge, pace and motivation**...' (these words are emboldened in the text) (OFSTED 1995a). This document and those on other subjects allude to problems of inspection in the section headed *Inspection Issues*. Wilcox and Gray (1995) note that although the *Handbook for the Inspection of Schools* (OFSTED 1994a) is comprehensive 'the OFSTED 'model' is now in the hands of a wide range of inspectors who will doubtless interpret and implement in somewhat differing ways, but they nonetheless, are assumed to play a common score.' This caution is not reflected in Rose (1995) nor the statement by a senior member of HMI at a recent seminar attended by one of the authors that the question of pedagogy is what the system must now be concerned with. OFSTED at this point has the confidence to make bold statements about pedagogy and the quality of teachers which are accepted by, for instance, the Teacher Training Agency.

The Agency's Chief Executive, Anthea Millet, recently said that raising the standard of entrants would be the agency's first priority, pointing to a finding by the Office for Standards in Education that 'one in ten new teachers is unsuited to the job' (Pyke 1995).

It would appear that OFSTED will be quite prepared to tread where HMI would not.

CHAPTER THREE

The Handbook for the Inspection of Schools: Models, Outcomes and Effects

by Janet Maw

Introduction

The *Handbook for the Inspection of Schools* (OFSTED 1994a) is an important text in that it interacts with the practices of inspection and the practices of schooling in complex and, as yet, inadequately understood ways. It is the chief means by which Her Majesty's Chief Inspector of Schools (HMCI) exercises his statutory duty under the Education (Schools) Act 1992 of giving guidance to those inspectors registered by him as fit and proper persons to conduct an inspection of schools.

Registered Inspectors (RgIs) are a primary audience for the *Handbook*, and it is clearly intended to act as a powerful means of control of the day-to-day practice of inspection. RgIs are required to adhere to its summary *Framework* as a condition for registration. Additionally, the *Handbook* is now in its third edition, and whilst this re-writing has been in part a response to subsequent legislation and other forms of regulation, and in part designed to increase the internal clarity and consistency of particular sections, its most noticeable outcome is an enormous expansion. RgIs have to familiarise themselves with nearly 500 pages of text, and this represents a formidable level of intended control. However, the *Handbook* is also the main focus in the training of inspection team members. Such training can, in fact, be described simply as training in compliance with the requirements of the *Handbook*. In addition, the open publication of the *Handbook* has meant that schools have also become an important audience for it (Coopers & Lybrand/OFSTED 1994, pp12–3), though it is not yet clear how widely dispersed any detailed knowledge of the *Handbook* is in the schools.

Given that the *Handbook* is, then, a powerful means of control with intended effects, but with different audiences and multiple interacting readings and responses, the rest of this chapter will attempt to address certain questions:

- What model of inspection does the *Handbook* present?
- What model(s) of schooling does it present?
- What are the outcomes of such inspection?
- What effects might we anticipate?

A model of inspection

I have presented a more detailed critique of the *Handbook's* model of inspection elsewhere (Maw 1995). Here I want to consider it in relation to three pairs of related characteristics:

- detachment and intermittence
- comprehensiveness and fragmentation
- qualitative observation and quantitative judgement.

The relationship between the inspection team and the school is one of hierarchy and detachment. Once the contract is agreed with OFSTED the Rgl is in charge of its implementation and the deployment of the inspection team, no member of whom should have had any prior connection with the school, its staff or its governing body. The inspection team has authority to attend all events in the school during the inspection period and to read all professional documentation. Whilst there are reports that some heads set ground rules for inspection teams (O'Connor 1995), these appear fairly marginal to the organisation of the inspection, and do not affect its nature at all. Staff have the right to correct factual errors at the inspection team meeting with school management prior to their meeting with the school governors, but:

> It is important that all who attend the meetings are clear at the outset that they cannot be occasions for seeking to modify the judgements which the inspection teams have reached, provided that these judgements are not based on factual inaccuracies. (OFSTED 1994a, Part 3, p21)

The emphasis on control and detachment presents the teachers as objects of the inspection process, not participants in it. The teacher is the 'absent voice' (Ball 1993, p108) in the inspection process. Moreover, whilst the inspection team may give feedback during the course of inspection, the inspection process provides neither advice nor support.

Once the school has produced its action plan following the report and had it approved by OFSTED it is likely to have no further contact with OFSTED until the next round of inspection, unless it is deemed failing or likely to fail. These characteristics of hierarchical detachment and intermittence are a political response to criticisms from the far right that HMI had acted in their own bureaucratic self-interest in ideological collusion with the schools (Hillgate Group 1986, 1987).

The *Handbook* is both comprehensive and extremely detailed about both *how* inspection is to be organised and *what* is to be inspected. The *Framework* for both of these is set out in Part 2 (36 pages) of the *Handbook*. Inspection organisation is further detailed in Part 3 (63 pages), whilst Part 4 (88 pages) expands the detail of what is to be inspected, and this is further expanded in the following section entitled Technical Papers (102 pages). Thus the *Framework* itself includes:

- 89 explicit 'criteria for evaluation', some of them multiple;
- 84 statements of 'additional evidence to include', some multiple;
- 76 statements of 'the report should include'.

Each of these is expanded in subsequent parts of the *Handbook*. For instance, the *Framework* includes one page on assessment, recording and reporting, which specifies four evaluation criteria. In Part 4 these are amplified into a half-page description of 'good practice' and an additional 18 evaluation criteria (OFSTED 1994a, Part 4, pp51–3). *Technical Paper 5* sets out the legal framework for assessment, specifies 25 further criterion questions and expands the presentation of 'good practice' (OFSTED 1994a, Part 5, pp37–46).

This acute fragmentation of the school's practices presented in the collection of data is mirrored in its reporting. Thus, in addition to much factual input/output data, largely supplied by the school, the Record of Inspection Evidence must include evaluation of each of the lessons and other activities seen, many further evaluation statements, and the judgement recording statements which contribute to the OFSTED data bank. For an 11–18 secondary school this requires nearly 1,000 judgement recording statements to be agreed by the inspection team, whilst for a primary school covering Key Stages 1 and 2 the number would be about 600.

Qualitative observation is mandated by the *Handbook* as the core inspection activity, the main means by which school processes are assessed. Whilst the *Handbook* presents many evaluative criteria to inform this observation it requires no systematic observation schedule in terms of frequency or sequence of events. Nor does it require any descriptive outcome similar to the ethnographer's field notes. What it does require is that all the qualitative observation has to be interpreted and recorded as quantitative ratings. This process begins with the individual lesson observation form (OFSTED 1994a, Part 3, p61), which provides for short evaluative statements on certain key features, together with a rating on a scale of one to five. Such lesson evaluations are then aggregated on the record of inspection evidence and used as the basis to complete the judgement recording statements (JRSs), this time on a seven point scale. The JRSs then form the OFSTED data base, which is used to provide the precise statistical information in OFSTED reports (e.g. OFSTED 1995a), a degree of precision which is quite unwarranted.

I have criticised this model of inspection more extensively elsewhere (Maw 1995) on the grounds of feasibility, validity, reliability, bias and control. Briefly, such doubts begin at classroom level, where it is assumed that grade descriptions such as:

1. Many good features, some of them outstanding
2. Good features and no major shortcomings
3. Sound
4. Some shortcomings in important areas
5. Many shortcomings

(OFSTED 1994a, Part 3, p16)

translate transparently from particular activities and practices to grade judgements. As a recent correspondent to the *Times Educational Supplement* put it:

> We know that each reader creates his or her own meaning when reading a text. OFSTED does not know this. It bases its whole edifice on the belief that the *Framework* will have the same meaning for all inspectors. (Bowring-Carr 1995)

Such problems are compounded by the successive levels of aggregation, which entail the belief that a meaningful consistency can be achieved in presenting hundreds of evaluations per inspection, by nearly 6,000 inspectors of different statuses (Coopers & Lybrand/OFSTED 1994, p4), in a context where over 6,000 institutional reports per annum are expected (OFSTED 1993a, p7).

Most pertinent to this discussion, however, is the fact that such qualities as validity and reliability cannot be subsequently checked for accuracy and fairness because no record of events and observations exists in any form other than evaluative. The accountability of the inspection team to those inspected is thus severely constrained. This raises the question as to how such a model of inspection may be conceptualised, and I want to argue that the characteristics outlined above are remarkably consistent with what Foucault (1979) described as a 'technology of power'.

Foucault argues that, increasingly from the late eighteenth century, systems of population control which depended upon visible and punitive forms of power, reliant on force and violence, came to be replaced by covert and regulatory forms dependent on systematisation, normalisation and recording. Such forms of regulation he called disciplines, which here have to be understood in both senses of the word, as fields of knowledge and forms of control, the knowledge–power nexus (Hoskin 1990). Foucault described such disciplines as operating in relation to a range of institutions, including the military, prisons, medicine and education. The defining characteristics of such disciplines, or technologies of power he saw as:

- hierarchical observation, whereby the objects of surveillance are made visible whilst the observers remain invisible;
- normalisation, whereby judgements are made by reference to a norm;
- examination, which combines the processes of observation and normalisation to produce a truth about the individual. (Foucault 1979, pp170–94)

If we substitute inspection for examination and school for individual it is not difficult to discern a correspondence between Foucault's analysis and the model of inspection in the *Handbook*. It is important to stress that Foucault saw such technologies of power as not simply recording a truth about what was observed, but as *producing* a truth through the interaction of knowledge, power and normalisation. Again, it is not difficult to see this operating in the model of inspection at all levels from the lesson observation form to school report to national reports (e.g. OFSTED 1995a). Moreover Foucault also described such forms of disciplinary power as 'moral technologies' in that not only do they produce a normalising truth about the individual/school, they also induce self-regulation in the observed through identification with the norm and the possibilities of gratification or punishment associated with particular judgements. There has been ample anecdotal evidence in the education press of such self-regulation by schools in forms such as attendance at in-service courses in preparation for inspection, which have proliferated, to trial runs of inspection based on the *Handbook* and often involving costly consultancy or LEA support. However, before we can speculate about the effects of this process it is important to assess whether the *Handbook* provides a model of schooling which can act as a reasonably unequivocal norm for self-regulation by schools.

A model of schooling

There is a degree of ambivalence in the *Handbook* as to whether the intention is to provide a model of 'good practice'. On the one hand there are a number of statements admonishing inspectors not to bring their pre-dispositions and preferences to bear in the process of inspection, e.g.:

> ... it is important that judgements about the effectiveness of teaching are based on its contribution to outcomes and not on inspectors' preferences for particular methods. (OFSTED 1994a, Part 4, p50)

> Judgements about [curriculum] effectiveness should be based on the standards of work and pupils' responses, rather than on predetermined notions of curriculum design. (OFSTED 1994a, Part 4, p55)

> Judgement about [management's] overall competence should be based on evidence, not just hunch or 'feel'. Attention should be focused on the quality of leadership and not on the choice of leadership style: there are many acceptable styles of leadership. (OFSTED 1994a, Part 4, p64)

On the other hand, such statements eschewing pre-set criteria must be set against the existence, within the five hundred pages of the *Handbook*, of many hundreds of explicit criteria, statements of good practice and criteria implicit in evaluative questions. Moreover, there are claims external to the *Handbook* that it describes best practice. Stating that over 10,000 copies of the document had been requested by 1993 OFSTED continued:

> Such a widespread distribution of the document, many copies of which have been requested by schools, is a start towards promoting best practice. (OFSTED 1993a, p8)

This ambivalence regarding pre-set criteria and models of 'best practice' has long been a feature of HMI self-presentation (Maw 1994, pp7–8), so its continuation into a text produced by HMI in OFSTED is not surprising. What is perhaps more important is to ask whether OFSTED is presenting a required model, a preferred model, or a range of acceptable alternatives.

The Education (Schools) Act 1992 lays a duty on Her Majesty's Chief Inspector of Schools to report to the Secretary of State on:

- the quality of education provided by schools
- the educational standards achieved in them
- the efficiency of financial management
- the spiritual, moral, social and cultural development of pupils.

Given these requirements, two features of the presentation of schooling within the *Handbook* do not appear surprising. Firstly, a strong element of normalisation is apparent. Manifestations of this include the frequent requirement to assess aspects of the school in relation to a range of legal and other regulations including the National Curriculum, health and safety legislation, the Code of Practice for special educational needs, religious education, etc. Inspectors also have to assess achievement standards against both national norms and in relation to pupils' assessed capabilities. In addition, of course, there is the normalisation process inherent in the quantitative judgement requirements. Secondly, the duty to report on financial efficiency means that sections of the *Handbook* are impregnated with concepts from the discourse of management (Ball 1993). Terms such as planning, efficiency, effectiveness and cost-effectiveness, resource control and value for money are deployed at the level of overall management, budgeting and resource allocation, but also in relation to the curriculum, teaching and classroom practice. Ball has argued that such a discourse of management, associated with a discourse of the market, leads schools towards forms of self-regulation in the interests of finance-led decision-making and competition with other schools (Ball 1993, pp111–2). There is a strongly bureaucratic thrust in the conception of good practice. Planning and recording are privileged attributes. In these features, then, the model of schooling presented is congruent with the model of inspection outlined above.

However, in other aspects, this is not the case. Each subsection of Part 4 includes an amplification of evaluation criteria, issues for consideration when reviewing evidence, and factors to be taken into account when reaching judgement. Taken overall these indicate the range, diversity, complexity and interactive nature of factors pertinent to judgements about schooling. They indicate a subtlety and perhaps tentativeness of judgement which is wholly belied by the crude reductionism of the rating scales presented in the model of inspection. They allow for variability of practice and present no precise model of good practice to which schools can tailor their activities. To this extent there is a degree of incompatibility (or, at the least, uneasy co-existence) between the fragmentation, 'objectivity', and quantitative judgement of the model of inspection, and the subtlety, variability, complexity and value-laden nature to be inferred from aspects of the presentation of schooling. Whatever the complexity and variability of good practice, the unquestioned assumption of the *Handbook* is that this will be unproblematically revealed by the inspection surveillance. Inspection is seen to recognise the truth, not to construct it. In summary, whilst there may be no easily discernible overall preferred model of the school in the *Handbook*, there are preferred elements, and these are strongly managerial. Again, this is reinforced by other OFSTED literature, e.g.:

> The *Framework* has been well received by secondary heads, who consider it to be a useful management tool. (Coopers & Lybrand/OFSTED 1994, p12)

Outcomes

There are three direct outcomes of the inspection process:

- the report to the school, together with its summary

- the record of inspection evidence
- the judgement recording statements which form the OFSTED data base.

Schools do not see the record of inspection evidence or the judgement recording statements. Indeed, in many cases they are unaware that the latter exist. Thus whilst the *Handbook* can be seen as a highly detailed technology of control, the report is a condensed set of judgements which functions to obliterate the means by which particular judgements are made.

The record of inspection evidence and the JRSs, on the other hand, are the mirror image of the *Handbook*. Together, through the presentation of a series of normalising judgements they constitute each school in 'a field of comparison' (Ball 1990a, p163) and through the aggregation process effected through the OFSTED data base produce a 'truth' about the system of schooling as a whole which hides the variable and subjective nature of its constituent parts behind the neutral, objective and scientific language of statistics (Ball 1990a, p164). Following an inspection a school has to produce an 'action plan' in response to OFSTED's report, but except in the case of schools deemed to be failing, there is no legal requirement for any external monitoring of the implementation of such plans. The responsibility for this rests with the governors.

Effects

The role of inspection, as set out in the Education (Schools) Act 1992, is to monitor the standards, quality, efficiency and ethos of the schools and to inform both the government and the general public on these matters; inspection demonstrates the *accountability* of schools. OFSTED, however, has claimed a role in the *improvement* of schools. Its first corporate plan was subtitled *Improvement through Inspection* (OFSTED 1993a), and an early report claimed that:

> Our intention ... is to do more than regulate; it is also to promote good inspections through improvement of the inspection arrangements and, above all, to provide a system and conditions which facilitate *school improvement*. (Coopers & Lybrand/OFSTED 1994, p35)

A later publication (OFSTED 1994g) offered a number of cases of schools which, it claimed, effected 'improvement through inspection', although it is clear from the reports that the process of inspection contributed little to the claimed improvement, which depended entirely on factors in the school context.

This question as to whether mechanisms of accountability can also operate as mechanisms of development and improvement runs through the literature on all forms of evaluation in and of schools. Hargreaves (1990) argues that such a reconciliation of evaluation roles has seldom been achieved in the past. He also claims that for inspection to act as an agent for improvement there must be a partnership between inspectors and teachers, and cites the ILEA *Inspectors Based in Schools* scheme as an example:

> A group of inspectors was freed of normal duties to spend their whole time in schools. They remained in one school for some six weeks. During the early part of their visit they talked with all the staff and observed lessons and other aspects of school life. They then immediately made a report to the school and their diagnosis and recommendations for change were discussed fully with the staff. The inspectors remained in the school to work alongside the teachers in implementing the agreed changes. The scheme was a remarkable success, perhaps not surprisingly, since it was itself a new form of partnership between teachers and inspectors. (Hargreaves 1990, p12)

The Further Education Funding Council (1993) has more recently set out a model of inspection incorporating characteristics of engagement, commitment, partnership, dialogue, negotiation and support within an ongoing cycle of inspection. The research literature on educational change, innovation and improvement (e.g. Fullan 1991; Rudduck 1991; Hopkins, Ainscow and West 1994) argues that such characteristics are essential to successful rather than superficial change programmes. This suggests that the characteristics of the OFSTED model, detachment, hierarchy, authority, intermittence and lack of support are not likely, in general, to lead to school improvement. For schools deemed good the model can lead to complacency, for schools deemed failing, the punitive nature of public exposure:

> ... often leads to defensiveness and denial rather than reform. And not surprisingly so; if you strip a man naked in public, his first reaction is not usually to pull up his socks. (Hargreaves 1990, pp10–1)

Thus, whilst it is impossible to predict the reaction of any one school to the inspection process, it would be flying in the face of much research evidence to suggest that the OFSTED model is likely to effect an overall improvement in the quality and standards of schooling. Can we, however, predict that it will lead to the self-regulated compliance, orthodoxy and homogeneity suggested by a reading of Foucault?

Here, I think, one must be much more tentative. A reading of Foucault would suggest a drab convergence of school practice over time, but Foucault, although he recognises the factor of resistance, concentrates more on the determining and normalising forces of technologies of power, largely because he focused upon them as systems and did little or no empirical examination of instances of them in operation (Fairclough

1992). To examine this question further I want to draw an analogy with the American concept of 'high stakes assessment', forms of assessment which determine curriculum and pedagogy rather than the other way round. Assessment is seen to be 'high stakes' if it is both demanding in terms of standards and the consequences associated with performance are important because they carry rewards or sanctions:

> The high stakes associated with test performance will force an instructional response to the test so that the test context will, in current parlance 'drive' instruction. (Airasian 1988, p305)

As Gipps points out:

> It is not that teachers want to narrow their teaching, nor to limit unduly students' educational experience, but if the test scores have significant effects on people's lives, then teachers see it as part of their professional duty to make sure that their pupils have the best possible chance they can to pass the test. (Gipps 1994, pp36–7)

One example of high stakes testing cited by Gipps is the nineteenth century system of 'payment by results', which had disastrously limiting effects on teaching in Britain. But that system, carried out by HMI, was also high stakes *inspection*. The question is then, whether the OFSTED model is also a high stakes form of inspection which will ensure the compliance of teachers. A point that Gipps emphasises in her review of American research is that it is the perceptions of participants which determines whether a particular form of assessment is high stakes, and that this perception derives from the political and social uses made of the outcomes. This raises the question as to whether schools and teachers perceive (and will continue to perceive) an OFSTED inspection to be high stakes or not.

The question is not easy to answer. The widespread evidence of self-regulation prior to inspection and much anecdotal evidence would suggest that they do, but we do not know the extent to which this is cosmetic. The short time-scale of events has allowed little evidence so far of the extent to which schools respond to inspection by further self-regulation, or whether the intermittent nature of inspection allows schools to ignore the recommendations. Nor do we know the extent and nature of schools' resistance to the process or how they assess its public impact. Moreover, whilst the system of 'payment by results' laid down clear and narrow criteria to which schools were to conform, the *Handbook* presents no such obvious model. On the other hand there is the possibility that pressures on RgIs and their teams will lead them to concentrate more on the preferred elements in the model of schooling, particularly those managerial aspects such as planning, efficiency and budgeting. Importantly, these elements mesh with the discourses of management and marketing which are also being imposed on schools by features such as local management of schools, competition for pupils, development planning, league tables and other performance indicators. Ball (1993) argues that the long-term impact of the use of such discourses and the practices they produce is to divide the teaching profession into an élite of management who control policy and planning and classroom teachers, increasingly seen as technicians or employees rather than professionals. In summary, the long-term effects of this model of inspection cannot be 'read off' from the *Handbook* itself, but will depend upon the developing web of belief, discourse and practice as it is implemented and perceived over time. Nevertheless we should note one principle drawn from an extensive survey of the impact of testing in the USA:

> The more any quantitative social indicator is used for social decision making, the more likely it will be to distort and corrupt the social processes it is intended to monitor. (Madaus 1988, quoted in Gipps 1994, p35)

Part Three: The Inspectors' Perspective

CHAPTER FOUR

'A fit and proper person ...' – The Training of Inspectors

by Carol Donoughue

> The Education (Schools) Act 1992 will lead to a radical reform of the system
> of school inspection, as promised by the Parents' Charter ... OFSTED will
> award contracts to Registered Inspectors. To be included on the register kept
> by HMCI an inspector must be judged a fit and proper person, and able to
> conduct inspections competently and effectively. He or she will be assisted
> by a team of inspectors. Registered inspectors and all their team members
> must have satisfactorily completed an appropriate course of training
> organised or approved by HMCI, unless they are specifically exempted from
> the training requirement. (DFE 1992c)

Even before the passing of the Education (Schools) Act a small group of
Her Majesty's Inspectors (HMI) was beginning to prepare for a total
reform in the inspection of schools. An 'opening up of the system' was
being promulgated by Conservative politicians and their advisers, and if
they were to win the forthcoming election, then the groundwork for
change would have to be in place. Instead of inspecting schools, HMI
were to become the trainers of inspectors and, ultimately, the monitors of
the quality of the inspection system.

Thus it was that in Autumn, 1991, HMI began drafting a *Framework
for Inspection* and making predictions about the numbers of inspectors
needed to inspect all the schools in England over a period of four years.
Their more problematic task was to devise a training programme for the
new style inspectors who would be required to start work in September
1993.

Coopers & Lybrand, in their review of the new system (1994) were
rightly impressed by the enormity of what had been required:

OFSTED was set a difficult task to set up a new approach to the professional task of school inspection; to set up totally new arrangements for delivering inspections; and to find and train a new cadre of inspectors to undertake the work. Furthermore all this had to be achieved at the same time as metamorphosing into a new organisation distinct from the former HMI.

In starting to consider models of training, HMI had little to which they could refer either in this country or abroad. They had in the recent past formalised their own year long induction programme. The new entrants, each in the care of a mentor, made a series of visits to different parts of the education system. They took part in inspections and were given increasing amounts of responsibility, until they could with some confidence lead an inspection team. They also attended a series of seminars during the year, which ranged over a variety of topics to ensure an adequate familiarity with different aspects of the system. The mentor, meanwhile, advised on report writing, communication with schools and with local education authority personnel. Clearly, this model, although thorough and wide ranging, was impractical for the new inspection programme.

Nor was there much to learn from the experience of local education authorities. Local authority inspectorates differ in the attention they pay to training newcomers. Most inspectors complain when asked, that they were expected to take up the reins on the first day of employment, as though the job was as easy as putting on a new coat!

At an early stage of their thinking, HMI considered the possibility of a fifteen day course for the new inspectors. There would be a three stage process which would gradually introduce the trainees to the newly written *Framework*, with tutorial days interspersed with 'field work'. This model, however attractive, had to be abandoned because it would take too long to train the number of inspectors required in the time-scale which had been set, and perhaps because it smacked too much of HMI training 'in their own mould'.

It was subsequently agreed that the stated objective of the training should be no more than to familiarise the trainees with the *Framework* and *Handbook for Inspection*, so that all inspections, no matter by whom they were carried out, would conform to the same pattern of inspection procedure and use the same criteria for arriving at judgements. It was also agreed that the training should last no longer than five days.

HMI knew that initially a substantial proportion of their trainees would be local authority inspectors and that eventually when that cohort had been trained a different training would be needed for a more varied group of professionals. They also knew that a sufficient number of secondary phase team members, registered and lay inspectors had to be trained and assessed to undertake the first round of secondary school inspections in Autumn 1993. There was some pressure therefore to finalise the training materials.

It was decided that the professional applicants would be able to choose to be considered for training either as team inspectors or as Registered Inspectors (RgIs). For the former a five day residential course was prepared; for the latter, the five day training was to be followed by inclusion as team member in an inspection led by HMI. Assessment would be an integral part of the five day course, and aspirant RgIs would be assessed by HMI included in the inspection team for that purpose. Similarly lay inspectors would receive a five day training with built in assessment tasks.

In July 1992, the DFE launched a £100,000 advertising campaign to recruit the 200 registered inspectors needed for the new inspections. The selection of candidates for training:

> ... took into account ... qualifications, teaching experience, management experience of inspecting and advising in schools and other relevant experience or expertise for the role. There was however flexibility within the guidelines to allow the non-educational applicant with appropriate skills to be selected for training. (Coopers & Lybrand/OFSTED 1994)

Nobody outside the section involved in the three stage process of administrative scrutiny, professional evaluation, and then further scrutiny by OFSTED personnel and an independent outsider could safely say how flexible the guidelines were. It certainly was the case that the first tranche of trainees was composed mainly of local authority inspectors, some former HMI (those who had already carried out inspections using the *Framework* were exempted from training), a few teacher trainers and a very few retired headteachers. Trainee team inspectors did not have to provide references along with their application forms, although those wanting to become RgIs were required to do so. The essential criterion for the selection of trainee lay inspectors was that they should not have taught in schools.

The trainers were initially HMI. They themselves had received a training to introduce them both to the content of the course, and to the criteria and procedures for assessment. There was a Tutors' Handbook which was to be followed to the letter, to ensure that every trainer/tutor with every group of ten or so trainees would provide the same training, using the same training materials at the same time and in the same way. The trainer became in fact the mouthpiece through which the training was delivered. No feedback was to be given to the trainees on their performance in the assessment tasks, no words of reassurance to those who, after the first day began to wonder why they had come. It was carefully explained at the outset, that although each trainer would be assessing the trainees in his or her charge, the final decision about success or failure would rest with a panel of assessors back at OFSTED, and ultimately with Her Majesty's Chief Inspector.

On subsequent courses successful RgIs were selected by HMI to be trained as trainers and gradually the numbers of HMI directing and acting as group tutors dwindled until the entire training process, both the residential component and the second stage training in schools (although not the final assessment), has been put out to tender to RgIs who are also accredited trainers. The training for lay inspectors was contracted out to accredited trainers from the start.

The five day course for team inspectors replicated as far as was possible the successive stages through which inspectors proceed in gathering evidence, coming to judgements about what they find, and conveying those judgements orally in feedback to the staff and to governors, and in a written report. Case materials, videos and simulations were used to replace the real experience of being in a school. Although the essential elements of the course remained the same for both secondary and primary phase trainees, there were of necessity phase-specific sections. When later secondary phase inspectors wished to inspect in primary schools, they were urged to take a two day 'conversion' course in order to feel secure in the different phase. However, team inspectors are allowed to inspect in either phase without taking the conversion course. It is only the RgI who must undertake this further training.

Throughout the five days trainees were required to complete tasks which were assessed according to criteria which were stated clearly in their course materials. The criteria for assessment were applied for both team and Registered inspectors and related to a set of competencies which it was hoped would be demonstrated during the five days and subsequently during the training inspection. They were:

Planning of inspection activity This means the ability to analyse data and written information and to identify the main features of whatever is being addressed and to draw out issues from evidence.

Management The ability to draw up an inspection strategy that will adequately address the stated issues, that is provide for the collection of the appropriate evidence within a realistic time-frame.

Professional knowledge and judgement The understanding and appropriate application of the criteria in relation to the lessons seen and notes of lessons provided; skills of analysis and synthesis, and the ability to come to sound judgements in relation to the evidence provided.

Oral communication This in particular requires clear delivery at all times, well-structured formal presentations and the ability to get the main messages across in a clear and succinct way.

Written communication Writing which meets the stated requirements, is clear and concise and draws out the main findings in relation to the available evidence.

The reactions to the course were understandably mixed, with those who failed feeling professionally vulnerable and, in many cases, too ashamed to admit in public that they had taken the training and been found wanting. A 'failed' applicant wrote to the *Times Educational Supplement* in July 1994:

> Two months later I heard in a formal letter that I had not been selected, no reasons were given, there had been no dialogue about the process, no professional accountability was offered, no redress, no way to feel satisfied by the overall experience.

On the other hand, there were several, who, whether they passed or failed – but usually if they passed – regarded the week, with its enormous pressures, and long hours, to have been an intense but rewarding assault course, even if they did not fully understand the criteria for their selection. The assessment criteria were clearly stated in the Students' Course Book, but trainees frequently complained that they didn't know what they were! Churcher (1994) reflected:

> It seemed to me that we were 'outsiders' trying to break into a secret society, and now, having become an official card carrying OFSTED team inspector, I still do not understand why I was selected and some others were not.

Some trainees dropped out in the middle of the course, when they realised that the demands that would be made on their knowledge of the National Curriculum, or on their ability to write fast and succinctly, would be too much for them.

The course for lay inspectors made similar and perhaps greater demands on the trainees. The lay inspectors by definition had not been involved in:

> the provision or management of school education, apart from voluntary involvement for example as a governor or classroom helper. (DFE 1993)

They were asked to absorb a quantity of information about the education system and about the issues which needed examining. They visited a school before the course and then for a day during the course. But perhaps the greatest problem for them was that insufficient clarification was offered to them about what might be the role of the lay inspector in the inspection team. One wrote:

> My own training course intake consisted overwhelmingly of middle-aged, middle-class, white men. Many, especially the few women, had experience as school governors. About half of us had industrial or business backgrounds; a

high proportion of us were full or part-time business or management consultants. I was one of the few with a background in education or training .... There was no indication that an independent voice was required, no recognition, even, that we might have a distinctive role to play. We were treated instead as old hands at a familiar game. (Letter to the *Times Educational Supplement* 1993)

By Easter 1993, there were 300 RgIs in the secondary phase and 1,000 team members, there were 70 primary phase RgIs and 500 team members, and 850 lay inspectors had successfully completed the training with a further 300 to be trained in the summer. By Autumn 1994, there were 500 secondary RgIs and 2,300 team members; there were 600 primary RgIs and 1,400 team members; there were 70 RgIs for special educational needs and 270 team members. (These latter had to have first completed the first stage training for either the primary or the secondary phase before taking a two day enhancement training for SEN.) A further 300 lay inspectors were about to be trained.

As had been forecast by HMI, the nature of the applicants for professional training began to change as the months went by. The numbers of LEA inspectors dwindled and the proportion of teacher trainers, head teachers, and retired head teachers grew. A number of the applicants, particularly the serving head teachers, applied for training not because they had the intention of inspecting, but because they saw the course as professional development and as a way of preparing themselves and their schools for the inevitable. This was particularly true of applicants for the primary training. Because the course had been devised for trainees who had previous inspection experience, the failure rate began to rise. According to an article in the *Times Educational Supplement* (October 1994) the head of registration at OFSTED admitted that:

the overall failure rate for primary five day training courses over the past 18 months was 25 per cent, but between August 1993 and April 1994 the rate increased to 38 per cent ... OFSTED said that the failure rate for its training course aimed at new secondary school inspectors was low, but it was unable to give a figure.

Not only were not enough trainees passing through the training, but there were not enough primary and special inspectors in the system already to inspect the numbers of primary and special schools which had to be visited over the next four years.

To compound the problem further, those primary RgIs who were trained, did not come forward in sufficient numbers to lead teams and work their way through the lists of schools which had been told to expect a visit in the coming terms.

In order to recruit the numbers of inspectors needed for present requirements, and to provide for a future generation it was necessary to attract not those already in inspection, as when OFSTED was set up, but those who had an increasing familiarity with the *Framework* and the *Handbook* – the heads and senior teachers of schools. Accordingly, the training had to be made more accessible, more attractive, and more appropriate for applicants who had no previous inspection experience, but who nevertheless would have to be seen as potential inspectors, if the 20,000 primary and 1,000 special schools were all to be inspected within the determined time span.

In September 1994, OFSTED put out tenders for a contract to write a new training course which would be more suitable for this different cohort of applicants. The course specification for the training for team inspectors required that there should be the opportunity for the trainee to determine how much of the content – the information about the different sections of the *Framework* – he or she needed to study. This content would be conveyed through distance learning packages. There would be a number of 'tutorial days' during which accredited trainers would concentrate on inspection skills – writing, making judgements, and classroom observation. Although trainees would have to complete course assignments as before, trainers would be able to give feedback – a notable difference from the original course. OFSTED was to be responsible for the final assessment of the trainees.

In Spring 1995 the new course was piloted. The trainees professed themselves delighted that their trainers could and did answer questions and were empowered to write helpful comments on their written assignments. However, they complained that the distance learning units took much longer to assimilate than suggested. They were, surprisingly, only required to make one visit to a school to practice classroom observation skills before they completed the course, and the opportunity provided by a two month time span to give adequate attention to perfecting their writing skills seems to have been neglected.

At the same time OFSTED became even more anxious about the shortfall in the number of primary and special school inspection teams available. The new training courses would only gradually produce the numbers of team and Registered inspectors which were needed, and there was no guarantee that those who had been trained would come forward to inspect in sufficient quantity. It was decided to offer a year's secondment to suitable candidates, who would, after an initial training and selection process, become team members as 'Attached Inspectors' (AIs), learning on the job.

> These posts offer considerable scope for career development and are particularly suitable for headteachers or deputy headteachers ...

ran the advertisement in the *Times Educational Supplement* in February

1995. The teams would be led by HMI. The AI will receive some form of training during the year, it is said, but this has yet to be determined at the time of writing.

The second phase of training to become a Registered Inspector was also to be changed. Inspectors aspiring to become RgIs have to submit a 'portfolio' of writing they have done for some five or six inspections. They also have to undergo a written 'examination' devised to test their knowledge of the *Handbook* and their ability to edit the writing submitted to them by their team members for inclusion in the written report. First reactions to this form of assessment have been of horrified amazement that there should be an expectation in one of the tasks that RgIs should know the *Handbook* by heart. The purpose of the task is in fact to discover whether candidates have internalised the main principles underlying the *Handbook*. Is this method of assessing the potential of team inspectors to be RgIs better and more reliable than assessing them on the job during an inspection? There is almost no way of assessing how an inspector behaves in the role of team leader, unless it is possible to observe a real situation.

Yet another problem facing HMI in OFSTED has been the constraints placed upon them by the Act in relation to in-service training for inspectors. They are only empowered – and given sufficient finance – to provide in-service training for RgIs, in the same way as they are only empowered to monitor the activities of RgIs. Team inspectors and lay inspectors go unassessed, and can continue without ever receiving further training. HMI provide five conferences annually to which RgIs are invited, and which serve as an opportunity to describe the latest changes to documentation, and to re-emphasise the need for sound judgements and evaluative writing. Because of the size of these regional gatherings it is almost impossible to respond specifically to individual needs, or to engage in any productive debate about the management of inspection in all its detail.

Although some attempts have been made to persuade professional associations to undertake in-service training for team inspectors, it has generally been left to contractors to arrange courses for them. Since there is no compulsion put on inspectors to attend, and since most inspectors, both team and lay, work long hours during the week, it is increasingly difficult to find times when they can and wish to involve themselves in further courses for which they have to pay. When they do attend, they are in the experience of the writer, still extremely concerned with the generic problems of handling the detail of the *Handbook*. Although they are attending courses on the inspection of, for example, English, or special needs, or technology, much of the discussion does not centre on those subjects, but on, for instance, how to write succinctly, how to make evaluative comments, where in the report to include comments which do not fit happily into one or other section of the *Framework*.

For lay inspectors there has been a different and for the most part unrewarding experience. One thousand were trained to take part in the earliest inspections. Not more than a half of that number have been employed, with the result that when they are invited to take part in inspection two years after their training, they have understandably forgotten much of what they learned during the five day course! Since many of them have derived little financial benefit from their initial training, they are even less willing to pay for in-service courses.

At the end of the first four-year period there will be a substantial number of OFSTED inspectors who have passed through one or other form of training, and who have, or have not, continued to be involved in in-service training. Will it be possible by 1997 to evaluate the effectiveness of the differing approaches to developing inspection skills and competencies? Have we trained inspectors to inspect, or have we trained them to follow the *Handbook* instructions? Is there a difference between the two? Are those Additional Inspectors who will have a year of on the job training, interspersed with tutorial time, it is said, more likely to succeed as inspectors, than those who have had either a five day residential course or a course, like the new training, interspersed with distance learning units? Ironically, there is a strong similarity between the year long secondment approach and the original HMI induction year!

There is no doubt that to have identified the competencies, and to have experimented with different models of training, is a major step which should stand a future generation in good stead, if inspection in its present form continues. However, those who have been and are being trained will experience a form of inspection and a rate of inspecting which may not in the end develop their expertise, or give them enough time to hone the more subtle interpersonal skills which are difficult to specify in a *Handbook*, which are not included in the competencies, but which are nevertheless an essential element of 'improving schools through inspection'. Hopefully a revised *Framework* and *Handbook* will allow inspectors more time in schools with less form-filling, so that they have opportunities for dialogue with staff, and reflection before they write. Hopefully after the completion of the four-year period, the pressures to inspect week in week out will be alleviated, so that inspectors have time to meet each other, to discuss, and to develop professionally alongside the schools they inspect.

CHAPTER FIVE

Inspecting by the Book

by Christopher Bowring-Carr

OFSTED published the first edition of the *Handbook for the Inspection of Schools* in 1993. Upon this document rests the whole of the OFSTED system of inspection because, as part of the *Handbook*, there is the *Framework*, which specifically sets out to tell inspectors how and what to inspect. This publication is therefore one of the most important documents that the educational world has received from Government since the changes to the system began with the Education Reform Act (1988). It is important for two reasons. The first is that it states the criteria by which inspectors are to carry out their work, and the statement comes in a document that is available to the public. The second reason is that by stating what the writers of the *Framework* believe to be a 'good' school, it provides a model for schools to emulate. In other words, the *Handbook* not only shows how schools are to be looked at, but it also states how schools should look.

The *Framework* needs, therefore, to be able to withstand very close scrutiny on three grounds. First, the language that is used must not be susceptible to multiple interpretations. Second, the list of obligatory tasks must be capable of being carried out by the teams of independent inspectors. Third, to take account of the diversity of schools and the contexts in which they are working and will be working, it is important that the *Framework* avoids presenting, implicitly or explicitly, a model of 'the good school' which is immutable. There is no reason why schools should be the only still points in society when all around there are profound social and cultural changes. It is the purpose of this chapter to demonstrate that the *Handbook* fails on all three counts.

One document, many readings

The main problem arises from the fact that the *Framework*, the obligatory part of the *Handbook*, has to reside in written language. However, written language is not immutable, and the meanings that people make from it cannot be guaranteed. One can only assume that the writers of the *Framework* believed that everyone would construct the same meaning as they read the document; in doing so they have taken up a Formalist stance. By Formalism I refer to the

> ... thesis that it is possible to put down marks so self-sufficiently perspicuous that they repel interpretation; it is the thesis that one can write sentences of such precision and simplicity that their meanings leap off the page in a way no one – no matter what his or her situation or point of view – can ignore. (Fish 1994, p142)

Fish, of course, as the creator of reader-response theory, goes on to demolish the above standpoint. Reader-response theory makes the Formalist thesis untenable. There is no such thing as a word that has a meaning which everyone will interpret the same way, no matter what his or her situation. There is no possibility of having a sentence from which all will extract the same meaning, regardless of his or her position. Every reader will create his or her own particular meaning from every act of reading, from every text. Reading is the creation of one's own meaning, not the reception of someone else's. The *Framework*, therefore, will be interpreted and reinterpreted, and as many meanings and emphases will emerge as there are readers. There will be no single meaning.

All the above is not merely playing the 'lit crit' game. After all, were we able to fix language in meaning for all readers and across time, we would not observe clerics quibbling with interpretations of holy writings and producing very different readings; we would not observe lawyers coming to very different conclusions in their readings of the law; we would not have critics finding different meanings in the poems and plays they had read. Once one accepts reader-response theory one realises that the idea that all inspectors will make the same meaning from their reading of the *Framework* is impossible. Profound consequences arise, the chief one being that there cannot be any standardised approach to schools, and, furthermore, no standardised outcomes.

Let me give an example. I am going to inspect English Literature and Language in a school. I will read the general sections in the *Framework*, and concentrate particularly on those sections that deal with teaching and learning. I will then read the 'text' of some 17 or 20 lessons, and respond to those texts by writing notes, and attaching grades on a 1–5 basis. There is absolutely no guarantee whatsoever that, if another English specialist inspector had read the *Framework* and sat through those lessons, similar notes would ensue with similar grades. Grades would vary; overall impressions of the work of the department would vary. There is no mechanism possible under the OFSTED system to begin the dialogues among and between inspectors which would lead to a diminution of these differences.

The concomitant to reader-response theory is the concept of the 'interpretative community'. If one takes reader-reception theory to its logical conclusion, there could be no shared meaning, no shared understanding. But the concept of the 'interpretative community' makes possible a shared meaning, arrived at over time and with a lot of discussion, by a community of people working and reading and talking together. In a staffroom, many of the key words used in assessing pupils, or in describing pupils and so on have equal resonances among most teachers. Over the years they have together been through a number of situations and discussions and arguments so that each knows the others' meanings and nuances, and each has edged closer to the others' reactions.

The working practices of OFSTED have been designed specifically to exclude the possibility of an interpretative community. Inspection teams and team leaders do not meet to share experiences and understandings. Subject specialists across different teams have no forum for sharing their knowledge and ideas. Those working in the headquarters of OFSTED read only what inspection teams have written but cannot meet the teams on a regular basis to know what they really mean by 'satisfactory' or 'efficient'. What we have is a large field in which teams of people are shouting words and numbers at each other, but no one knows what the others are hearing. The idea that someone can then say that 'x per cent' of lessons are good or poor is clearly untenable.

Metaphor

I would like now to turn to another aspect of the language of the *Framework*. The *Framework*, like every text, operates on metaphor. Through a careful look at the metaphors one can discern how the writers are trying to influence the readers, and, perhaps more importantly, what the cast of mind was of the writers.

Let me take a very small example. In Section 5 of the *Framework*, there is the section on 'Pupils' personal development and behaviour', a section to which I will be returning later. It begins with:

'Spiritual development is to be judged by the extent to which pupils display:
● a system of personal beliefs, which may include religious beliefs.'

It is very difficult to understand how, first, we are to interpret the idea of inspecting the development of a young person's spirituality. In all of the definitions in the dictionary of the word 'development', the idea is of a change taking place over time. One such definition is, 'a gradual unfolding or growth'. In our everyday use of the word, whether we are referring to a part of a city going through 'development', or to a skill being 'developed', or to a nation moving from poverty to a more 'developed' state, there is an implicit idea of change over a period of time. 'Development' of any sort cannot be critically evaluated in the three or four days inspectors are in a school.

It is equally difficult to understand how this process of development, if it can be said there is one, is 'to be judged'. The passage goes on to give external markers which, they say, will show that 'spiritual development' has taken place.

I have a number of problems with this idea. The first comes to me from Macbeth:

There's no art to find the mind's construction in the face.

Furthermore, whose spirituality is being used as the reference point? Some claim that the suicide bomber dying for his or her religion is the purest manifestation of spirituality. There is nothing in the *Framework* that says what sort of personal beliefs pupils should hold. Nor, of course, could it. The lack, however, means that it is up to each individual inspector to decide whether this or that system of personal beliefs is a sign of spiritual development, and such a judgement, of course, derives from the inspector's own set of personal beliefs and value system.

Second, I simply cannot believe that, given the ways in which inspections are carried out I could make any 'judgement' on pupils' spiritual development. As an inspector, I will sit at the back of some 15 or more classes, see, for the most part, the backs of the students' heads, and listen to what they have to say in response to questions and comments during an English lesson. These comments may be answers to questions about grammar and syntax, the structure of a poem, the unfolding of a plot. From this patchy and superficial observation, I am supposed to make a 'judgement' as to their spiritual development, which implies, *inter alia*, that I have some idea of what their spiritual state was before they came to this school and into contact with this teacher. It is stretching the powers of the inspector to breaking point to think that she can trust the pupils' 'display' of internal, complex, evolving matters such as 'personal beliefs'. Such a demand invites the inspector to play God.

Post-modernism and uncertainty

I have taken some time so early in this chapter to look at the metaphors in a very small passage because I believe that this section is a very good example of two flaws in the *Framework*. The first is that the writers continually use metaphors from concrete, visible aspects of life and apply them to very nebulous, complex aspects of life trying, by so doing, to give an impression of solidity, the idea that one can look at, say, a class and make judgements which are certain and reflect the reality of what was going on.

The second is that in their choice of metaphors the writers display a cast of mind which is set in the modernist era, in a time of certainties and of continuities. We, however, and our colleagues in schools and our children live in the post-modernist age. We live in a world in which there are only situational certainties, not scientific ones; we have no belief that outside of where we are there is a permanent 'reality' against which we can set what we think we have seen or heard or experienced. There is no fixed metre rule against which to measure our impressions. This document is written for a past age and has little relevance for the one in which schools are living.

One example brings home clearly the world in which the writers lived at the time of writing, and also of the fundamental impossibility of carrying out all the demands of the *Framework*. Section 5, as I have noted above, deals with the pupils' personal development. As one would expect, there is a deluge of the sonorous words with which to play the 'spiritual development' game, such as: 'Search for meaning'; 'awe and wonder'; 'respect for persons'; 'responsibility and initiative' and so on. However, there is also an assumption that there can be certainties in this area. 'The extent to which pupils display an understanding of right and wrong'; 'reasoned judgements on moral issues'; and then in a note towards the end of this section 'intimations of an enduring reality'; 'in relation to what is right or wrong'.

As with so many sections of the *Framework* one is torn between being overwhelmed by the sheer impossibility of fulfilling the demands placed upon one as an Inspector, and a feeling of hopelessness that such rigidities and certainties could be contained in a document dealing with the education of young people at the end of the twentieth century. In the time inspectors have in a school, it is entirely unreasonable to think they could get to know children intimately enough to gauge if a pupil feels 'a sense of awe and wonder', or if a judgement on a moral issue was based on the workings of reason.

Inspectors are supposed to gauge a pupil's 'growing understanding of society through the family, the school and the local and wider communities'; this is an impossible demand. How do pupils 'display an understanding of the difference between right and wrong'? Whose moral code is being used as the measuring rod? If a pupil does not do anything 'wrong' during the days of the inspection, is that pupil displaying an understanding?

The note at the bottom of the page tacitly admits the impossibility of completing this section. 'Spiritual development relates to that aspect of inner life through which pupils .... It is characterised by reflection, the attribution of meaning ... valuing ... intimations ...'. It would be a bold, if not downright foolish, inspector who would be prepared to venture into the inner and most private aspects of an adolescent's mind.

Code of conduct

The *Framework* opens (page 3) with a 'Code of conduct'. In paragraph 2, the principles which should govern the conduct of inspections are specified, and, as one would expect, the list contains all the right words: 'objectivity', 'fairness', 'sensitivity', 'evidence', 'judgement'. These are, of course, the counters that you would expect to use in the game of inspecting. They have the right timbre to match the seriousness of the game. The problem is, however, that here as elsewhere, the words float free of any context outside the *Framework*. The words and their meanings are imposed by the hierarchy, the writers of the *Framework*. These are the words of the priesthood who set the meaning, who set the context. It is a patronising, top-down vocabulary.

As I have tried to indicate above, these words attempt to give solidity to what is a very tentative business. If I am to be an inspector, I am to be 'honest in framing and communicating ... judgements.' There is no suggestion here of the immense difficulties involved in being an observer, translating what you think you might have seen and heard into another medium – words on a page. There is no suggestion of the difficulties in transmitting that imperfect rendition of what you might have seen to another person, especially if that person was the observed who thought she was doing something else. There is no suggestion of the immense difficulty of communicating that impression to an unknown outsider, and then not knowing what impression she or he got from your now very attenuated piece of writing.

No – there is only the ringing certainty that inspectors are honest in communicating their judgements. As I have said, the *Framework* reduces, over and over again, a very complex and tentative business to ringing assertions of certainty.

There is a further problem. Inspectors are instructed to come to corporate judgements. Teams will reach corporate judgements through discussion and, on occasions, through compromise. Let us consider the situation in which seven of the team consider that an aspect of the way that senior managers go about their work is satisfactory and the eighth does not. To achieve the corporate judgement, the eighth has, at some point, to give way and agree with the majority. Is that inspector being honest?

Another word from paragraph 2 (i) is 'consistency' – the inspector is to be consistent, but at what point did this consistency set in? In the 'Introduction: Using the Handbook', paragraph 1, we read that the 'purpose of the Handbook is to provide guidance which will help develop ...'. Does the notion of consistency fit easily with that of development? Surely, if I am to develop there must be at least the possibility of my discarding one set of attitudes and developing another. Furthermore, 'consistency' and 'sensitivity' are uneasy bedfellows; if I am going to be sensitive to a number of different situations, I am going to be changing according to those situations and therefore inconsistent. 'Inconsistent' is not necessarily a bad thing; to apply a rule 'consistently' can be very unfair indeed as most of us can remember from our school days.

'Judgements' (used twice) and 'evidence' are used as if they are absolutes, words having meanings which overarch human vagaries and differences. There are no such absolutes.

And finally – 'objectivity'. Objectivity is not possible. To ask someone to be objective is to ask her to step outside her personality, to cast aside all memory, all learning, all experience, all that goes to make self. It is simply not possible; if it were possible, what you would get was a robot waiting to be programmed. Equally, of course, you cannot be subjective. To be subjective, you would be continually reacting to stimuli, not filtering them through experience; you would be, not to put too fine a point on it, insane.

The demand that inspectors be 'objective' is indicative of this 1930s/1940s mindset which is obvious in so many parts of the *Framework*. There was once a belief that a scientist could stand outside the box, peer into it without in any way altering what he saw, and then report on the 'reality' that he had observed, and his personality would in no way alter, influence or direct that reporting, or the questions that he had originally framed to get the report. The idea that the observed should work with the observer, and that reports that emerge would be tentative, joint, and multi-layered, simply do not impinge on this *Framework* at all. It is as if we are still in the '30s, the age of certainty, and, of course, of rigid social layering. We will inspect the school, we will be honest and objective; you will be inspected, and we will tell you what we have seen and form a judgement as to how good or bad you are.

The writers demonstrate a masculine view of reality, depending as it does on external rather than internal inquiry, and they claim that right because they feel they are validated by the hierarchical systems in which they work. There is nowhere in the *Framework* any indication that we live in a culture of uncertainty.

There is, however, a glimmer of hope. We need to read at this point, the Inspection Schedule: Guidance, Section 5.1 C, page 18:

> no subject-matter is value-neutral, even those which most aspire to objectivity of treatment. Indeed, it is a crucial part of moral development to understand that this is so.

A different hand at work?

What is a school?

I would like to look next at another problem the writers appear to have. Oddly enough, it is over the word 'school'. At different places in the *Framework* it takes on different meanings. In the Introduction (1.1) the word 'school' is used in an accustomed and ordinary way – the report has to contain information about the school, such as its type and status, where it is situated, its DFE number. Here the word is being used in a routine, bureaucratic way; the school is an institution which can be characterised by certain standard designations.

Then, in 1.2 we begin to detect a slight shift.

> The report should include: a description of the nature of the pupil intake and those features of the area served by the school which influence the work of the school.

There are many oddities about this demand. 'The nature of the pupil intake' – what, precisely, does this mean? That the pupils are, by and large, well off and well fed? That they come from two-parent families, in the main? That they are ill-fed and come reluctantly to school? What is meant by 'the nature' of the pupils? And how can the inspectors, who do not know the area or the children, in the brief time they have in the school, make more than a most superficial, and because superficial, misleading comment? As inspectors are not ethnographers, they will not be able to do more than give a label to the area: 'The children come from an area characterised by owner-occupier homes, with few signs of deprivation.' This is not a description, except in the most superficial way, and it raises many questions. Is the fact that the children come from owner-occupied homes implied to have an effect on the expectations of the inspectors as to the standards of work that they will see? Does it have an effect on the behaviour that will be expected? The risk is, of course, that the necessarily abbreviated description will lead to stereotyping.

But the problem does not stop there. The inspectors have to comment on those 'features of the area served by the school which *influence the work* of the school' (my emphasis). The inspectors now have to sift through all the features of the area, analyse the work of the school, show how some features affect the work of the school, and others do not, and then comment on how the work of the school would have been different had the school been in a different, but unspecified, location. But then, of course, it would have been a different school.

Once again, the *Framework* makes a facile demand. It reduces the complex matter of the interaction between the pupils of a school, the teachers, the parents, the expectations that have, historically, been held of what education can or cannot achieve, and a lengthy list of other variables, to a simplistic and unachievable demand.

But to return to the word 'school'. At the beginning of the introduction it was a bureaucratic institution, with a number and a 'type'. Now, however, it is something which does some work, and this work can be influenced by the area it 'serves'. The bureaucratic institution takes on some animation. Pupils are not part of it, however. The school 'intakes' the pupils and does some, as yet unspecified, work 'on' or 'to' them.

On page 22 (Section 5.1) there is the phrase, under the heading 'Evidence should include', 'a: observation of all aspects of school life'. Now, the school has a life, and that life includes lessons in which, clearly, there are pupils. At this point, the idea of 'school' *does* include pupils. Then comes: 'c: the influence of the school's aims ... on the pupils' development'. Here we have the school having aims and policies and codes of conduct and so on, and all these impact on the pupils, who are, again, not part of the school except in so far as they are affected by it.

At 'h:' the pupils make 'contributions' to the school; they are on the periphery; if I make a contribution to a charity or the work of an organisation, I am not a part of it, though I wish it well and want to help it.

Finally, at 'j:' we find that the school makes a contribution to spiritual, moral, social and cultural development – but it does not state whose development is being looked at.

The confusion continues: 'the pupils contribute to or restrict ... the quality of life in school; the functioning of the school as an orderly community.' Surely pupils do not 'contribute' to the community; they *are* an essential part of the community. In fact there would not be a community at all if the pupils were not there. What is developing is a clear attitude to the concept of school. Mainly, it is seen as a bureaucracy doing things to pupils (the work of the school). Pupils receive, and occasionally 'contribute to'. They are not a part of.

One is reminded of the stories of one's youth, stories of the days when there was an Empire and the Regiment went out to uphold the honour of

Queen and Country. Then, the regiment had an existence over and above and not dependent upon individuals. The regiment could do no wrong; only individuals could, and if an individual transgressed the rules he (and this world was singularly masculine) was expected to 'do the right thing' and the loaded revolver was picked up and used. Individuals could 'contribute' to the regiment, but the regiment was a living being apart from and above them.

Unfortunately, the problem over what the writers think a school is does not end here. In Part 4 of the *Handbook*, which is a section of guidance, on page 63, there is a set of notes which purports to amplify the criteria which are used to evaluate the management of a school.

The section starts with the clause: 'Where (*sic*) a school is well managed ...'. We appear to be back to the idea of a school being a bureaucratic institution, and indeed in the first sub-section we read 'where the school should be heading' and 'the school's current and future situation', both being consistent with the idea of an institution.

In the next sub-section, though, we see again the phrase 'the school's work' but it is the governors, the head teacher and the senior staff only who give 'a clear direction' to it. The remainder of the staff merely play a role in the running of the school, and, if they are fortunate, they have their contribution (that distancing word again) appreciated. Pupils contribute nothing – they 'learn effectively and efficiently'.

However, four sub-sections on, everyone (governors, staff, parents and pupils) has 'a strong commitment to the school'. The writers seem unable to have one clear, consistent picture of what a school is, what the term 'school' comprises. As with so many of the key words in this document, the meaning shifts in and out of focus, adding to the miasma of different interpretations that its readers will create.

Conclusion

The *Handbook* demonstrates very clearly the insurmountable problems inherent in an inspection system.

1. The writers have used language as if meaning could be fixed among readers and over time. Meaning cannot be so fixed.

2. Judgements cannot, therefore, be standardised within or among inspection teams.

3. As there is no forum for teams to meet, as teams or in subject groups, there is no long-term prospect of there being established an interpretive community which could begin to mitigate the worst effects of the *Framework*.

4. It is a document emanating from a hierarchy, with those being inspected having no part in its framing. Therefore, any discourse is unbalanced, with those inspected always having a weaker position in any disagreement.

5. The *Framework* covers, in very great detail, every possible aspect of a school. The demands that it makes in total cannot be met by inspection teams. Outcomes are, therefore, partial.

6. The report that emerges is a report on a still photograph and not on the process of education in a school.

7. As the *Framework* is the instrument of a bureaucracy, change will be slow and reluctant. At a time of very rapid change in all other aspects of life, this inertia works against the best interests of schools.

8. The *Framework* assumes there are certainties independent of time, situation and people. There are no such certainties.

There was a time when the idea of being inspected by a group of people who neither knew your school or had any responsibility for it was acceptable. That time has passed. The inspection of a school by a group of people who have no stake in the long-term betterment of that school cannot any longer be justified. We are no longer in the sort of society in which that hierarchical structuring can be sustained. Further, we know that change and improvement comes not from externally issued dictats but from slow and steady work initiated and sustained from within the institution. Finally, we know that the OFSTED system is not concerned with quality assurance; it deals in control. It is a part of the struggle of a central bureaucracy to attempt to ensure that schools operate according to a set of rules laid down at the centre. It is part of a wider struggle waged by dying bureaucracies against the inevitable loss of their power.

CHAPTER SIX

OFSTED: A Registered Inspector's View

by James Learmonth

The approach to school inspection which was reflected in the Education (Schools) Act 1992 and in the setting up of the Office for Standards in Education (OFSTED) came as a shock to many school inspectors, both in Her Majesty's Inspectorate (HMI) and in Local Education Authority (LEA) inspectorates. In the late 1980s we knew that radical change was coming: the Education Reform Act of 1988 had given LEAs new responsibilities in the monitoring and evaluation of the National Curriculum, and in the same year the Secretary of State, Kenneth Baker, made it clear that the Conservative government intended an enhanced role for LEA inspectorates:

> The local inspectorates will need to monitor and evaluate school performance. They will need to provide LEAs and the schools themselves with trusted and informed professional advice, based on first-hand observation of what schools are actually doing, of the way in which they are implementing the National Curriculum, and of the standards achieved. (Baker 1988)

LEAs began to develop their inspectorates, welcoming a model which linked evaluation with 'trusted and informed professional advice'. Some LEAs had already been involved in joint inspection with HMI, and the potential of combining the local knowledge and continuing responsibilities of LEA inspectors with the more objective and national experience of HMI seemed a powerful impetus to school development. Some HMIs, including myself, were attracted by the prospect of the new balance of evaluation and support inherent in the new arrangements, and took up inspection posts in an LEA. So why did the Government then change direction?

The Government made its view clear in a White Paper that LEAs had not moved fast enough:

Previous local authority inspection arrangements in some areas were shameful – irregular and unsystematic visits followed by unpublished reports with little or no evaluation. A report by the Audit Commission in 1989 *Assuring Quality in Education: a Report on Local Authority Inspectors and Advisors* was damning, and rightly so, of the school inspection service in many local education authorities (LEAs), depicting a system in disarray without clear policies or guidelines. Inspectors in some areas were reported to be spending as little as 3% of their time in the classrooms; too often there was no clear distinction between inspection and advice, so that sometimes inspectors told schools what to do and then checked up to see if they were doing it – rather than their proper task of evaluating whether or not it worked. Although there has been some improvement since 1989, it has been too slow and uneven. The Government could not let this continue. Hence, from next year, all schools will be subject to regular and rigorous inspection under the watchful eye of the new and powerful Chief Inspector of Schools. (DFE 1992a)

The other origin of the new inspection arrangements was the Parent's Charter of September 1991, which pledged access for parents to open inspection reports on all schools, so that their choice of school could be informed by clear, up-to-date information. Such reports would also 'demystify' the process of education, and be without the jargon now associated with educators. A lay inspector in each inspection team would bring common sense to their deliberations.

Most school inspectors wish to believe that their work makes some contribution to raising standards in schools and improving the quality of educational provision. Going back to basics, they recall the first *Instructions to Inspectors* (1840) in which the Committee of the Privy Council for Education insisted that:

... it is of the utmost consequence that you should bear in mind that this inspection is not intended as a means of control, but of affording assistance: that it is not to be regarded as operating for the restraint of local efforts, but for their encouragement. (Committee of the Privy Council for Education 1840)

More recently, the functions of HMI were defined as:

1. assessing standards and trends, and advising the Secretary of State on the performance of the system nationally;
2. identifying and making known more widely good practice and promising developments, and drawing attention to weaknesses requiring attention;
3. providing advice and assistance to those with responsibilities for and in the institutions in the system through its day-to-day contacts, its contributions to training and its publications. (HMI 1990)

Under the Education (Schools) Act 1992, HMCI retains the broad statutory duty to keep the Secretary of State informed about standards of achievement, quality of education, efficiency of management of resources and the development of values in schools.

In summary, OFSTED's new inspection arrangements appear to have three main purposes:

1. to collect information about standards in schools so that Her Majesty's Chief Inspector of Schools is able to make an annual report to the Secretary of State;
2. to provide information about individual schools so that parents may make informed choices;
3. to improve the quality of provision in schools.

The Government also wanted the nature of the relationship between inspector and school to change. HMI were seen as too remote and theoretical, often peddling the latest trendy ideas to, presumably, gullible teachers; and LEA inspectors often described themselves to their schools as 'critical friends', thus bringing upon themselves calumny for having too 'cosy' a relationship with schools. The Secretary of State in 1992, John Patten, envisaged a new breed of inspectors as 'big cats prowling on the educational landscape.'

HMI were left with the task of designing, quickly and with little consultation, a framework of criteria which inspectors would use in making their judgements on each school. As an HMI working in schools I made judgements drawing on criteria implicit in HMI publications, short courses and internal conversations, both formal and informal. It was never entirely clear whether as visiting HMIs we imported into a school a set of consistent values about good practice in teaching and learning, or whether we accepted the school's value system and reported on how successfully they realised their own objectives. As an LEA Chief Inspector, I negotiated first with heads and deputies, then with governors, a set of criteria by which the schools in that LEA wished to be judged. As an OFSTED inspector, I welcomed the explicit criteria set out in the *Framework for the Inspection of Schools*. I was aware, and hoped that schools were too, that open and consistent criteria for judgement did not necessarily bring with them consistent interpretation of the criteria by inspectors.

Contributing information to OFSTED

As a registered OFSTED inspector, I believe that the current arrangements enable me to deliver the quantity of information which Her Majesty's Chief Inspector requires. The various inspection documents – Lesson Observation Form, Subject Evidence Form, Judgement Recording Form, etc. – provide ample quantitative data in a manageable form for judgements about standards to be made, both in respect of individual schools and nationally. But I share the anxieties of those who are concerned about the quality of this information. The very amount and simple categorisation of the data may give them spurious credibility. OFSTED is aware of the problem, and clear where responsibility lies:

> OFSTED recommends more effective monitoring by RgIs of team inspectors' work ... in many of the early inspections RgIs did not monitor lesson observation forms sufficiently and intervene when necessary to ensure that they were consistently reliable. (OFSTED 1994e)

There are situations when RgIs can detect, for example, a lack of match between an inspector's comments and the grade awarded, or between an inspector's comments and the criteria set out in the *Framework*. But OFSTED's comments assume a consistent reliability between different inspectors' judgements which is likely to be achieved only after far more extensive training for individual inspectors than OFSTED requires or inspectors' professional circumstances (or the lay inspector's personal circumstances) permit. Furthermore, the *Framework* requires so intense a schedule during the period of inspection that, particularly with a large group of inspectors each of whom has his or her own specialist subject, little can be done on the spot to develop the consistency which would enable the group properly to be called a 'team'. The results of OFSTED's monitoring of the reliability of judgements in a school inspection is valuable for RgIs in the medium or long term, but comes too late to bring reassurance that a particular group is making judgements in a school which would closely match those made by a different group in the same school, or those made by a different group in a similar school elsewhere in the country. The RgI has a duty to ensure that judgements about a particular school are 'corporate'. In the sense that the general conclusions are agreed by a group of inspectors who have come together, often for the first time, to work together during the week, this is usually possible to achieve. In the sense that the judgements are those of a 'team' (the word used in the *Framework*) – a group which has had time to develop a collective identity, with consistent understanding and interpretation of evaluative criteria – there must be considerable reservations. Whether applied to the individual school or nationally, targets for improvement which include a rise in the number of lessons graded at a particular level ('sound', 'good' or 'very good') assume a national consistency for which there is little evidence.

Much has already been written about the quantity of paperwork required by OFSTED centrally. It is certainly frustrating for RgIs to spend days accumulating data and text which are not of value to the school and which may or may not be put to efficient use elsewhere. Such requirements may take so much time that the RgI has to skimp on other tasks.

Providing information for parents

I welcome the increased involvement of parents in school inspection. The Parents' Meeting before the inspection has usually been fruitful in questions for further investigation during the inspection, and most RgIs seem not to make the mistake of assuming that parents who attend the meeting are 'representative' of the parent body as a whole. More generally, the meeting provides an opportunity for parents to find out more about the process of inspection, and for inspectors to gain further knowledge of parents' perspectives and priorities. Writing the final report with parents in mind as prospective readers is a good discipline for RgIs, and the new format for report summaries, suggested by OFSTED in 1995, is more accessible, more representative of the whole report and thus much to be welcomed. However, OFSTED's insistence that each school is to be treated as a discrete entity, rather than in the context of both LEA and national policies, is not helpful to inspectors seeking to present parents with a comprehensive and accurate picture of a school's performance. It is frustrating for a RgI when a school makes the case that LEA actions have had a particular impact, positive or negative, on its performance and it is not possible to contact the LEA for confirmation, denial or amplification. It is clear from inspection evidence that there are now, for example, a number of secondary schools in inner-city areas which find themselves competing with grant maintained schools for intake at Year 7, and then being asked to take into later years, often Years 10 or 11 when GCSE courses are in progress, pupils who have been excluded from these (and other) schools. If the inspection report is confined to one school, it is difficult to present to parents a coherent, full and balanced picture of all the contextual factors, though these are likely to be known to professional educators working in that local area.

Improving the quality of provision

It is in relation to this purpose of inspection that I as a RgI feel most frustrated. It may be that the current arrangements for inspection do not comprise an effective and cost-effective method of school improvement, as Hargreaves (1995) suggests. Much of the research on school-improvement makes it clear that school-improvement is a complex and time-consuming process, rather than simply an exercise in making judgements and expecting the institution quickly to remedy its exposed weaknesses. The evidence suggests that some continuous co-operation between a school willing and able to evaluate its own performance, and an external 'agency' which is sympathetic in its response to the school's needs, is most likely to be successful. An OFSTED inspection, reflecting as it does the sharp separation of inspection and advice, doesn't seem to fit the bill, and may be counter-productive. We must find a more constructive balance between pressure and support.

A RgI has little time to reassure a school community about the purpose and conduct of the inspection beforehand. There are opportunities to meet the Head, staff and governors beforehand, but what remains in most teachers' minds is the rhetoric with which the new inspection arrangements were launched, and the nagging possibility of being designated a 'failing school'. These are not conditions which encourage teachers to give of their best, and a small minority of head teachers consciously or unconsciously contribute to what is sometimes rising hysteria by overemphasising the demands which an OFSTED inspection is likely to make of a school, or by making sudden and unreasonable demands for more policies to be written. During the week of the inspection, with a clear and full agenda set out by the *Framework*, a RgI is pressed for time to convince teachers that inspectors are genuinely looking for the school's strengths and weaknesses, or for evidence that the staff is one which reflects on its practice and constantly explores new possibilities for improvement, rather than a group hell-bent on completing its audit-sheets before the end of the week. If there is time for feedback about individual lessons, it is usually superficial and one-way, rather than the extended discussion about curriculum content or teaching approach which both inspector and teacher may want. It is through such discussions with teachers and pupils that inspectors can build a picture of whether what is happening in the week of the inspection reflects what normally happens in the school. (Most of us have had comments from pupils such as 'Can you come again next week please? We do very interesting work when you're here.')

It takes time, and experience of the whole school working normally, to assess the 'culture' of a school, and to work out where what Joyce (1991) calls the *doors to school improvement* may be found. Agreeing the judgements is feasible at the end of the hectic week, but often they are those already expected by the school. If these point out weaknesses, they are by definition problems of which the school has been aware but has been unable to solve. Or they are those which seem to be said about most schools anyway: the need for more differentiation of the curriculum, for example, or for middle managers in secondary schools to take responsibility for monitoring and evaluating provision within their own area of responsibility. The difficult process is that of supporting the school in its efforts to change or improve, but the OFSTED team by this time has disappeared, and although an LEA representative may (or may not) have been invited to the governors' meeting to hear the *Key Issues for Action*, there is no opportunity for the LEA (or any other agency) to discuss with the OFSTED group how these improvements might take place.

The situation may be particularly acute for schools judged to be 'failing'. For a few such schools it is possible that a public humiliation is the catalyst needed to prompt the school community into remedial action. For many more, it is an official stamp of 'failure' on a community already exhausted and demoralised by its own difficulties. RgIs must comply with statutory requirements and do their best to ensure that their judgements and practices conform with the procedures specified for identifying 'schools requiring special measures', but it is unrealistic to assume that such judgements are consistent across inspection teams, even granted OFSTED's 'checking' visit. And it is desperately difficult, and of course a huge waste of financial resources, for a RgI and the team to walk away from a school so designated. The judgements came free; the action plan is relatively straightforward to design; the necessary advice and support to make changes will be expensive. The process of change is likely to be painful, messy and time-consuming, with the school needing all the support it can get from experienced and knowledgeable sources.

What is needed is a much more coherent relationship between school, LEA and inspectorate so that support can be provided earlier in the process and certainly before the crunch of an OFSTED inspection. All schools should be involved in continuous self-evaluation, supported if necessary by the LEA or other external agency, as part of their quality assurance programme, rather than fixing their gaze on the visit of OFSTED inspectors as quality control. The Government has encouraged, or at least tolerated, the development of this approach in Scotland. The present Secretary of State, Gillian Shephard, has spoken positively about the need for schools to be self-evaluating institutions, and it may well be that, under either a Labour or Conservative government, that's the direction in which school inspection will go.

Whatever the arrangements, the current provision for training RgIs and other inspectors is quite inadequate. This is a matter of quality. If the three main purposes of school inspection are to be realised, and schools, parents and Government are to benefit from accurate and consistently reliable information, far more time and imagination needs to be devoted to the format and content of training. The process initially labelled 'training' by OFSTED has in reality been an 'assessment of suitability' process for individual inspectors. There are no regular opportunities for subject inspectors to compare and refine their interpretations of evaluation criteria, or to develop national consistency. The position is even more difficult for inspectors allocated the responsibility of covering such important and sensitive aspects as equal opportunities or efficiency of the school, either on an ad hoc basis for one inspection or intermittently over a period of time. While the practice of inspection is undoubtedly strengthened by the involvement of both lay inspectors and school-based educators, it would be ironic if inspectors are required to continue to make judgements about the quality of information made available to decision-makers in schools, without being confident that the judgements and information for which they are responsible as inspectors are not of the highest possible quality.

CHAPTER SEVEN

Lay Inspectors: Insiders and Outsiders

by David Hustler and Valerie Stone

Introduction

> 'I've enjoyed it very much, I think it's a great privilege to go into a school, to wander into someone's class and to sit there and be nosy ... I have not felt on any of the inspections that people have looked down on me or that I was an also-ran.' (Lay Inspector)

Over the last year and a half, a team at the Manchester Metropolitan University have been researching into the experience of the Lay Inspector within the OFSTED inspection process. The Lay Inspector is defined as:

> ... a person without personal experience in the management of any school or the provision of education in any school, (otherwise than as a governor or in any other voluntary capacity); and whose primary function on the team is not that of providing financial or business expertise. (DfE 1992b).

At least one Lay Inspector has to be involved in each inspection team and it is a source of continuing surprise to us that almost two years after our research started and the new OFSTED inspection system got underway, we can still find very little systematic research looking at Lay Inspectors. The absence of research in this area is particularly surprising given the controversy in the education establishment which surrounded the notion of Lay Inspectors when first introduced, a controversy which has certainly been a source of concern for some Lay Inspectors themselves as the following statement makes clear:

> '... perhaps you do not realise how vulnerable Lay Inspectors are. Ted Wragg has through the Times Ed. done a pretty good hatchet job on Lay Inspectors. The teaching profession will gleefully wait for the butcher, the baker and

candlestick-maker (all on zimmer-frames of course) spouting "Guv, string 'em all up" or "That's nice, luvvy", waiting for the Lay Inspector to commit a faux pas.' (Lay Inspector)

The quotation at the start of this chapter, from a Lay Inspector, might further fuel parts of that controversy centring upon the dangers of 'amateurs moving in on a hitherto sacred territory' (*Guardian*, 7 September 1993), though we should note that our research suggests that the 'wandering' is in fact very carefully organised from the point of view of all parties. The introduction of the Lay Inspector was heralded initially by government as being an important aspect of the Citizen's Charter, whereas some might regard it as a part of a continuing attempt to undermine the professions (Hargreaves 1994). Given this, one might have expected more research on Lay Inspectors to have developed.

Our own research started with the Lay Inspectors themselves, through an extensive questionnaire sent to over 200 Lay Inspectors trained in the north and north-west of England, and through a series of interviews and follow-up interviews. We have also interviewed 17 secondary head teachers, all of whom have experienced inspection and we are also able to draw on the perception of Registered Inspectors (with a total experience of well over 200 inspections) through questionnaire and interviews. We have had considerable help in our work from the Association of Lay Inspectors (ALI), based primarily in the north. We have already reported on aspects of that research (Hustler, Goodwin and Roden 1995), and in so doing have discussed a variety of issues relating to who the Lay Inspectors are and their involvement in the inspection process. In brief, the majority of practising Lay Inspectors are male (though, as we note later, female Lay Inspectors have a better chance proportionately of being involved in an inspection); they are about 51 years old on average and are largely self-employed/retired; they come from professional backgrounds mainly, are well qualified and there is a leaning to the educational, financial and manufacturing sectors (though bearing in mind part of the original controversy involving Kenneth Clarke, then Education Secretary, regarding whether or not your local butcher should be involved as a Lay Inspector, we should note that we have also encountered one ex-butcher).

Our work has pointed to some initial concerns about the lack of support some Lay Inspectors felt they received in early inspection work (and yet, from another perspective, the extent to which some Registered Inspectors felt Lay Inspectors needed too much support). In addition, many Lay Inspectors were surprised at the absence of any mechanism for feedback from the Registered Inspector or others concerning how they had done within the inspection, and a few had not even seen or been asked to comment on the final report. Things do seem to be changing here, as experience of inspection is developing and OFSTED is attending to some of these issues. However, Lay Inspectors continue to find certain difficulties in performing some tasks, not least relating to the different modes of organisation across differing Registered Inspectors, and several are still surprised at the lack of review on their own performance. We have also reported on the typical framework allocations for Lay Inspectors, with clear winners being: behaviour and discipline; community links; spiritual and moral development and attendance, (but we have noted the considerable degree of variation regarding what the Lay Inspectors are becoming involved in). It is apparent that many Lay Inspectors would welcome the opportunity to move beyond a central concern for only a limited number of *Framework* areas. Several, for example, express an interest in 'efficiency' because of their previous experience. Overall our research suggests that the vast majority of practising Lay Inspectors have found the work very demanding but 'very worthwhile'.

Any one of the above areas or issues and many others we have on record concerned with the practising Lay Inspector's experience of inspection, could be pursued in much more detail and might have provided the substance of this chapter. There are several clear specific matters with implications for improving the mechanics of the inspection process. However, our intention here, perhaps surprisingly, is to focus, initially at least, on those Lay Inspectors who are not practising, who have not been involved in inspection work, since it is our view that there are considerable, if somewhat neglected, matters here which require attention and some action. We believe these matters go to the heart of what we might mean by the very notion of the Lay Inspector. In the following section we present some of the data bearing on selection and non-selection, primarily drawing on comment from Lay Inspectors themselves. The final section leads us into a more general discussion relating to this data and some additional materials, together with certain recommendations for taking things forward.

Becoming a practising Lay Inspector: the neglected, the turned off and the safe bets

'I have written to OFSTED requesting a list of independent agencies who are contracting for work but I have had no reply. I feel that Lay Inspectors have been very much left to fend for themselves .... It may have been more useful to train people as the work became available.' (Lay Inspector)

'I am also concerned that education seems to be a bit of a 'closed shop' and it's not *what* you know, but *who* you know. I am sure Registered Inspectors are 'searching out' their friends to be part of their teams.' (Lay Inspector)

It is fairly well recognised now that there has been, and continues to be, a problem for many Lay Inspectors in getting inspection work (*Times Educational Supplement*, 10 June 1994). Our own interview and questionnaire work with individual Lay Inspectors points to a considerable degree of frustration here, linked to a variety of speculations as to why they have been unable to secure inspection work, whereas others they know have. More about these speculations later. A national survey of Lay Inspectors by the National Association of Lay Inspectors (NALIS) suggests that of the 1,235 Lay Inspectors contacted, almost 50 per cent still awaited their first invitation to inspect a school. From our own more limited sample of 200, over 40 per cent are in the same situation. Comments from some Lay Inspectors themselves, working and not working, as well as comments from Registered Inspectors we have interviewed, suggest that they believe this is due to 'OFSTED having got their logistics all wrong' and 'It's a question of oversupply, which may gradually ease', together with considerable sympathy being expressed by some Registered Inspectors and several working Lay Inspectors.

The matter might be left there, with some sympathy, given a view that it is the practising Lay Inspectors we should be focusing on. However, it is our view that this issue of not finding work merits further exploration and sheds some light on how the OFSTED enterprise is functioning in the market context. Let us look at a few comments from Lay Inspectors.

> 'Having waited and tried for up to two years to go on to an inspection team, I am now completely 'switched off.' (NALIS questionnaire data)

> 'Originally I had the impression that Lay Inspectors would find it easier to get involved ... I thought the commercial development side took something away from the notion that an ordinary person could get involved.' (Lay Inspector)

> 'I went into it with a sense of duty and public-spiritedness, not as a career. I am not inclined to chase after jobs ... it was not my perception that we would be thrown on the job-market and have to chase for jobs.' (Lay Inspector)

> 'My motivation originally was my interest as a governor in education ... I didn't even know it was to be paid at the time. I came away enthusiastic, pencil-sharpened and then the work was not there.' (Lay Inspector)

> 'It's flogging a dead horse. When I went into it, it was as a consultant expecting a reasonable rate for the job. Oversupply and rate-reduction has been the problem. There were a lot of 'incestuous' links with educational people which helped exclude a lot of the more business-like people like me.' (Lay Inspector)

Some of those trained initially have clearly given up trying, primarily it seems because of their lack of success. There are some other interesting comments as to why some have been 'turned off'. The middle three extracts above are not untypical of a number who came through training full of enthusiasm, but never realised that they would have to sell themselves in quite this way; who brought, they would argue, a desire to put something back in and a public-spiritedness, but found a market environment they never anticipated. By contrast, the last interviewee found that the increasingly depressed state of the market, in terms of the rate for the job, was not to his liking and not worth the candle, given his need to secure a decent overall consultancy income.

All five of these interviewees are no longer actively seeking Lay Inspector work, and their comments point to features of how OFSTED inspection is functioning both as a very competitive market and in terms of a market where rates are being forced down.

There is another well-known factor influencing selection.

'I'm worried about the balance ... felt there was too little scope for a male Lay Inspector. The lack of women subject inspectors may have kept me out of other inspections as it was an easy thing to fill the Lay Inspector's place with a woman.' (Lay Inspector)

Our own data suggests clearly that if you are a female trained Lay Inspector then you do have a better chance of finding work than a male. Registered Inspectors, Lay Inspectors, ALI and NALIS recognise this issue, which is seen to be associated with OFSTED requirements for team gender balance.

'Most of the Lay Inspectors I have worked with are female because this helps to make up the overall gender balance of the team.' (Registered Inspector)

Approximately twice as many men as women, overall, have been trained for Lay Inspector work and this issue of gender 'discrimination' is a sore point with many, appearing several times in our interview work. Perhaps we should refer to the suggestion of one Registered Inspector that the Lay Inspector should be taken out of the gender balance equation.

There are then a large number of Lay Inspectors, trained as such, but unable to find inspection work. However, where Lay Inspectors had been successful in finding work, their experiences had generally become enjoyable and fulfilling, and their views on the inspection process were very positive.

'Inspection has now become a full-time career for me, which pays relatively well. The work is enjoyable and not overly demanding.' (Lay Inspector, over 20 inspections completed)

'I've done eight now and feel that I'm really getting on top of the work, though every school is different.' (Lay Inspector)

But:

'I haven't done any more since the two I did right at the beginning, so I feel I'm in danger of getting rusty and I have been trying to get on more contracts.' (Lay Inspector)

Turning things around, we need to consider just how Lay Inspectors *are* being selected for work. Some of the above quotations provide a few speculations here (and the gender balance matter is obviously one influencing factor). Comment from our interviews and questionnaire work with Lay Inspectors and Registered Inspectors is quite illuminating here.

> 'Two had been trained by a colleague and had been recommended, one came via a mutual friend, one I met at a conference.' (Registered Inspector)

> 'I now tend to stick with two ladies, one of whom is a full member of my team.' (Registered Inspector)

> 'Many Lay Inspectors are the wives or husbands of educationalists.' (Registered Inspector)

> 'The one I use a lot is one of my neighbours.' (Registered Inspector)

> 'It's important, I guess, to know who are safe bets ... who are reliable and are not going to pursue some strange line of their own.' (Registered Inspector)

The general picture increasingly seems to be that where the Registered Inspector has been involved in the selection, it has been done on the basis of personal contacts and recommendations from others. As experience builds up, agencies, LEAs and Registered Inspectors are relying on those who have proved reliable, a safe bet, etc.

> 'Talking with other Registered Inspectors makes it clear that there are some appalling Lay Inspectors and some very good ones ... the message seems to be that when you get a really good one, you should hang on to him or her and not tell anyone else!' (Registered Inspector)

Clearly, particular Lay Inspectors have built up track records, for better or worse, and agencies and LEAs have been developing pools of Lay Inspectors who have inspected and whose performance is known about. The OFSTED register barely gets a mention as a source of assistance when putting together a team, though many Lay Inspectors have got into the system initially through their own mail-shot contacts with Registered Inspectors, LEAs and agencies. Registered Inspectors noted more broadly that their general criteria involved ensuring that the selection matched both the school and the balance of the team (including gender), that they did look for previous involvement in education (especially as a governor) and that religion, ethnicity, ability to write clearly and concisely and their previous professional background were also relevant factors, some more so, for particular bids.

Not surprisingly our own research seems to provide some support for what some might refer to as a developing 'closed shop' and 'incestuous' links with educationalist speculations, which earlier quotations referred to. We return to this issue in the next section. Our research suggests that, overall, many Lay Inspectors are not doing any inspection work, quite a few have done one or two inspections (and several of these are finding it difficult to get more work) and a relatively small number of Lay Inspectors are really doing quite a lot of inspection work. Some of the latter are clearly making virtually a full-time career of it.

In addition, it is our understanding that many schools, within a single LEA, are now being grouped together by OFSTED in groups from two up to fifteen and over. Tenders to inspect these blocks of schools are filled within a limited list of named inspectors for inclusion in the inspection teams. These may include one or more Lay Inspectors. This means that if the tender is successful, the block of schools will all be inspected by those named on the tender. It is likely that these Lay Inspectors will have ample work. It means, however, that often other Lay Inspectors will find it even more difficult to gain employment. In addition, the guidance relating to the Lay Inspector being contracted for at least 10 per cent of in-school inspection time will in itself not involve more Lay Inspectors.

Lay Inspector: outsider or insider?

What might we take out of the above then? Firstly, there are a large number of people who responded enthusiastically to the original invitation to become Lay Inspectors, who in many cases seem to have been motivated by an interest in education, a concern to 'put something back into education' and general public-spiritedness, who were even more enthusiastic at the end of their training programme ... but who have been unable to find work. There are also many who anticipated easier access to work and better rates for the job as part of a consultancy portfolio. As we will suggest shortly, one of the reasons why some may have been unable to find work is precisely because they had little experience of education or contact with educationalists, and yet the notion of the Lay Inspector was built on this being their strength! This is a key issue which we will shortly pursue.

One point we would wish to make here is that there is a group of trained, but not employed, Lay Inspectors who increasingly feel neglected and 'turned off'. The question we pose concerns whose responsibility it might be to relate to these neglected aspiring Lay Inspectors and are there any mechanisms through which they should have a greater chance of being used? The answer to the former would seem to be OFSTED; the answer to the latter is more problematic but deserves some attention and may hinge in part on the following discussion.

One major issue here relates to the educational experience, knowledge and contacts of practising Lay Inspectors. Our own research suggested that at least regarding our sample of Lay Inspectors, several came from a professional background within education anyway (e.g. Higher Education or LEA work) and that those who had such a background were more likely to be involved in inspection. In addition, those who had had more recent experience of education in one way or another were once again more likely to be involved in inspection (particularly if they were governors). It is also useful here to draw briefly on our research with head teachers who had experienced inspection in their schools. A general perception from head teachers was that their original fears and apprehension regarding the Lay Inspector role were not justified. In brief, experience had removed almost any element of hostility, and half our sample were fulsome in their praise of the Lay Inspector. Of those who remained sceptical, most felt that their own Lay Inspector had made a valuable contribution, even if they remained agnostic about their necessity. It may not be entirely by chance that in two thirds of our sample of schools, the Lay Inspector brought with him or her considerable experience of contact with education and/or schools. In brief, is it all that surprising that initial fears regarding Lay Inspectors, fuelled by the early press controversy, have not been realised? Not only does Lay Inspector work seem to have become the domain of the professional middle-class, but additionally, many practising Lay Inspectors are pretty conversant with educational matters.

As noted earlier, we are also building up a group of Lay Inspectors with a considerable experience of inspection and this might be reinforced by the block tender developments. The question which some are putting (Lay Inspectors themselves, but also Registered Inspectors and others) is to what extent considerable experience as a Lay Inspector begins to cast doubt on what we might mean by 'lay'.

'I am a bit worried about losing the freshness and the independence elements that a Lay Inspector can bring, once they have done too many inspections.' (Registered Inspector)

'At present I feel I am remaining 'lay' and am not too influenced by the professionals.' (Lay Inspector)

'It is an issue here, how often you are a Lay Inspector and become 'tainted' and therefore stand to be influenced by the professionals, and lose your amateur status.' (Lay Inspector)

What appears to be happening then is that increasingly the processes through which a school finds a Lay Inspector on its doorstep have, not surprisingly, led to that person, in all probability, having either had considerable experience of education themselves, or considerable experience of operating as a Lay Inspector, or being familiar with educationalists through everyday social interaction and discourse (and quite likely some mix of all these three). This begins amongst other things to raise some fundamental questions concerning what the generic role of the Lay Inspector is, should be or could be, given the personnel emerging as practising Lay Inspectors. What the generic role of the Lay Inspector should be has never been all that clear, but comments from Lay Inspectors and others are suggestive:

'He was the best of the team. It was good to have an independent presence.' (Head teacher)

'It is a great way of making sure that the professionals and experts do not bamboozle people and that they have to explain it in lay terms.' (Lay Inspector)

'I think we are a sort of check on the rest of the team.' (Lay Inspector)

'Our key job is on the communications side ... to unpick the jargon.' (Lay Inspector)

'We can ask the naive questions which the professionals are unable to.' (Lay Inspector)

'I value their freshness and their capacity to pose questions as an outsider, from Joe Public's point of view.' (Registered Inspector)

According to our research, a large number of Registered Inspectors and head teachers place some value on these dimensions of the role, yet for Registered Inspectors of course when push comes to shove, their preference is for a safe and effective team with a 'safe bet' Lay Inspector, rather than risking a Lay Inspector who is unknown to them (no matter how 'fresh'). It is the 'safe bet' of course who, it can be argued, may increasingly be losing aspects of that freshness and that independence, who may be absorbed into the jargon rather than be able to unpick it. If the aspects of the generic role pointed to above are to be maintained, then it may be that OFSTED need to consider some changes to the system.

We should point here to the mixture of meanings associated with Lay Inspectors as 'insiders' and 'outsiders'. One sense here is the straightforward one concerning those who are practising and are 'inside' the system, contrasted with those trained but unable to find work and still waiting in the wings. As a research team we are not carrying any particular brief for, or arguing the case for, those trained but not working. There is, however, a connection between this situation and a central theme in this chapter. This concerns the extent to which a number of factors may be leading to practising Lay Inspectors increasingly becoming *cultural* 'insiders' within the educational system. This of course seems to conflict with some of the original notions concerning the distinctive contribution which Lay Inspectors can make and interestingly enough it is also a matter of concern to some Registered Inspectors and head teachers regarding what they have come to value about the Lay Inspector role. We will close with a few tentative suggestions for amendments to the system.

There are a number of possibilities for change, some of which may be problematic in their implications, whereas others would seem more feasible, and necessary, in order to meet some of the concerns captured in our research *if* they are also concerns for others! This has demonstrated clearly that a proportion of the time, money and commitment expended both by Government and by a willing army of original trainee Lay Inspectors has in part gone to waste because of the number who have failed to gain employment. Skills learned in the initial training programme have lain fallow and knowledge is in danger of being lost or superseded. One possibility which could act as 'pump primer' might be for OFSTED to guarantee each Lay Inspector one initial inspection soon after the formal training. Though perhaps difficult to implement, this would raise the morale of the Lay Inspector population, offer a forum for practical application of skills learned and knowledge acquired, and would require that teams make use of a broader range of Lay Inspectors. This possibility might, however, not only seem impractical from a number of points of view but also not in tune with current market philosophies.

It might, however, seem important to retain the autonomy of those teams bidding for contracts, whilst clearing the ground for other Lay Inspectors to gain employment. A more viable set of interdependent proposals might be for OFSTED to limit the number of days per year that Lay Inspectors could spend on school inspections or limit the number of inspections per year. The research suggests that some Lay Inspectors have created almost a full-time career. The spirit of the original legislation, as some perceived it, suggests that there was no intention that this should be so. The corollary is also to raise questions about notions of being 'lay' and the ability of such 'inspection focused' people to retain their 'outsider' Lay status. In order to meet this concern OFSTED could consider including, amongst its criteria for accepting bids, one which would discriminate in favour of tenders where, for the Lay Inspector, it is a first inspection, or allocate more points the fewer the inspections undertaken by the nominated Lay Inspector. Furthermore, tenders for teams which can demonstrate that they use a wide range of Lay Inspectors could receive a higher grading by OFSTED. These latter proposals would seem to be logistically possible and would meet some of the arguments from our respondents in favour of such changes, not least that they would help to reduce the concerns about lack of employment and the worries shared by a number of the participants, that Lay Inspectors need to operate within a variety of contexts, of which school inspection is only one.

Furthermore, some of those interviewed felt that the 'green shoots of impropriety' were springing up and there is some anecdotal evidence of Lay Inspectors being recruited on the basis of long-standing friendship with Registered Inspectors. These sensitive issues could be moderated considerably if at least a package of proposals along these lines was adopted by OFSTED.

In the domain of equal opportunities there is clearly some bitterness amongst trained Lay Inspectors with little or no work, about the requirement that inspection teams should be gender balanced resulting often in the frequent use of a small number of female Lay Inspectors. In order to extend employment opportunities across a wider group, OFSTED might require that the gender balance of the team be considered without reference to the sex of the Lay Inspector. We merely draw attention to the suggestion which some respondents have made, and we recognise that this might be problematic given the large numbers of men who have been trained to be Registered and team inspectors. There is some evidence, however, that this picture may be regional rather than national.

Finally, we should make it clear that our research also suggests that some Registered Inspectors and Lay Inspectors who are fully employed feel strongly that a small number of Lay Inspectors is preferable, since these people through their experience, have become extremely knowledgeable and competent in the field. There is some reluctance to alter the status quo. There is a fear here that these skills might be lost in spreading the work more thinly and including more and less experienced Lay Inspectors. Here of course we revisit fundamental ironies revolving around the concept of the Lay Inspector. There is a connection here with a point we touched on earlier relating to feedback to the Lay Inspector. Many Lay Inspectors were uneasy about the quality of their performance on early inspections. Only rarely was a formal debriefing offered by Registered Inspectors. It is self-evident that a constructive debriefing would help to boost the performance of Lay Inspectors on subsequent inspections. Registered Inspectors, short of time and using a small group of Lay Inspectors have no incentive to provide such feedback. Only a formal mechanism, with a clear and positive set of criteria, would ensure an entitlement of the Lay Inspector to an accessible evaluation of their practice. At the same time, however, such a requirement would contribute to the more rapid and coherent development of Lay Inspector skills and would possibly enable the extended cohort of employed Lay Inspectors to become more competent and more of an asset to the Registered Inspector and the inspection team, or at least to gain some understandings relating to why they may not be invited to participate in subsequent bids! Although we have expressed the above in Lay Inspector 'entitlement' terms, it might be more productive to develop a simple procedure and format for a post-inspection *exchange* of information and perceptions between the Registered Inspector and the Lay Inspector focusing on the process of the inspection, serving in part a quality control function and available to OFSTED. Possibilities along these lines have been suggested to us by some respondents. Such an approach signals the distinctive roles of the Registered Inspector and the Lay Inspector within an inspection team and would certainly add another dimension to conceptualisation of the Lay Inspector as a significant 'insider/outsider'.

Closing on a somewhat different note we should also point out that several of our Registered Inspector and head teacher respondents expressed support for the notion of the 'community inspector'. One study which did seem to have informed early Government thinking about Lay Inspectors stemmed from an HMI visit to South Australia in 1992. The preface to this report (HMI 1993) noted that:

> 'HMI sought to identify countries where the use of 'lay' inspectors already exists in order to obtain evidence about the likely roles and functions of such persons. The closest parallel was found in South Australia ...'.

There are, however, some crucial differences between the two systems: in the South Australian system the 'community member' is chosen jointly by the school and the community through a short-listing process, is likely to be well-known to the local community, is not paid and is almost invariably a parent and most likely to be a mother not engaged in paid employment. Any movement in this direction would of course add a whole set of new meanings to that term 'insider' and would obviously require a drastic reconceptualisation of the notion of the Lay Inspector as it has developed to date. We merely note the continuing interest amongst some of our respondents in this very different model.

CHAPTER EIGHT

Value for Money: How Schools are Assessed by OFSTED

by Rosalind Levačić and Derek Glover

The requirement to inspect efficiency and value for money

The Education (Schools) Act, 1992, added a new dimension to the work of school inspectors by including the 'efficiency of the school' as one of the four major 'aspects' upon which the school is inspected by OFSTED and requiring inspectors to make a summary judgement on the value for money provided by the school. In devising 'the efficiency of the school' part of the *Framework for the Inspection of Schools* OFSTED (1993d) drew upon the expertise of the Audit Commission, which was thus able to extend to schools its mission of promoting in the public sector the economic-rationalist approach to management with its criteria of efficiency, effectiveness and value for money. This model is alien both to traditional administrative bureaucracies and to professional carer cultures which characterised schools prior to local management. This culture is still highly valued by educational professionals who are having to adapt to new criteria by which the success of schools is to be judged.

In this chapter we consider how the concept of value for money and the related criteria of efficiency and effectiveness have been interpreted and applied to schools through the OFSTED inspection framework. An extended report of the research is available in Levačić and Glover (1994). In this we chapter we address four key questions:

1. How have the criteria of efficiency, effectiveness and value for money been interpreted and applied by OFSTED?

2. What kind of judgements have inspectors made about value for money and how do these relate to their assessment of efficiency and effectiveness?

3. Are inspectors' value for money judgements influenced more by their assessment of the educational effectiveness of the school or by financial considerations?

4. In what ways could the OFSTED *Framework* for inspecting the 'efficiency of the school' be clarified?

In order to address these questions we first analyse the OFSTED *Framework* for the evaluation of the efficiency of the school against standard definitions of the key concepts of efficiency, effectiveness and value for money in economics and in public sector accountancy. The second part of the chapter draws on an analysis of 66 inspection reports taken from a wide range of secondary schools inspected in the Autumn Term 1993. The sample consisted of:

Type of school	Age	Total number of schools	Single sex
Comprehensive	11-18	30	3
Comprehensive	11-16	20	3
Comprehensive	13-18	5	
Comprehensive	9-13	1	
Grammar	11-18	5	4
Secondary Modern	11-18	5	1

How have efficiency, effectiveness and value for money been interpreted for application to schools?

OFSTED's guidance

OFSTED's *Handbook for the Inspection of Schools* provided the first clear official explanation of what is involved in the efficient and effective management of resources by schools. It brought together financial management and school development planning which up to then had been addressed somewhat separately in the official guidance (DES 1988; The LMS Initiative 1988; Hargreaves et al. 1989; DES 1991a).

The guidance on evaluating the efficiency of the school (OFSTED 1993c, d) is somewhat complex. At the heart of the efficiency assessment are four main criteria upon which inspectors are required to report.

1. The standard of financial management and planning.

2. The efficiency and effectiveness with which resources are deployed to attain the school's aims and objectives and to match its priorities.

3. The effectiveness of financial control.

4. The assessment of any steps taken by the school to evaluate its cost effectiveness.

It is significant that these four criteria do not directly correspond to the standard definition of efficiency, which is a comparison of outputs with inputs, but are strongly process oriented. The standard definition of efficiency as set out by the Audit Commission (1984) is securing the 'minimum inputs for any given quality and quantity of service provided'. Efficiency by itself does not imply that resource use is thereby socially optimal. To make such a judgement requires that the output be valued. Any attempt to define one particular combination of goods and services as having more social value than some other combination inevitably implies a value judgement about the distribution of income associated with each combination of goods. Efficiency in the sense used by the Audit Commission (i.e. cost efficiency as opposed to allocative efficiency, see footnote to Table 8.3) is therefore restricted to meaning that a given quantity of output is produced at the least possible cost: it does not imply anything about the social value to be attached to that output.

In contrast to efficiency, effectiveness is a concept which embraces an implicit, if not always explicit, assumption about the social value of output. The standard definition of effectiveness (Audit Commission 1984) is 'how well a programme or activity is achieving its established goals or other intended effects'. The separate definitions of effectiveness and efficiency mean that a programme can be effective but not efficient or efficient but not effective. A third 'E' also features in public sector audit; this is 'economy' defined as acquiring resources in the 'appropriate quality and quantity at the lowest cost' (Audit Commission 1984). The three Es come together in the concept of 'value for money' which embraces economy, efficiency and effectiveness. However, as Glynn (1987, p48) notes 'value for money's a phrase with wide and ambiguous meaning.' He proceeds to define it in relation to a department or programme in which 'those who strive to provide the service do the best they can with the resources that are available'. Thus there are two distinct definitions of value for money used in public sector audit. One is in terms of outputs compared to inputs and requires both efficiency and effectiveness. The second is in terms of process and requires evidence that resource managers engage in market search in order to secure the best value purchases (i.e. practise economy) and evaluate what is purchased against the needs of the organisation.

Applying the standard definitions of economy, efficiency and effectiveness requires quantitative measures of outputs and inputs. However, the various outputs of schooling are either not quantifiable or where they are, such as examination results, require good quality comparative data and sophisticated statistical analysis. Such value added measures of examination results are not yet nationally available. The difficulty of obtaining data for the measurement of the standard definitions of efficiency and effectiveness explains OFSTED's emphasis on process rather than output/input indicators for assessing the 'efficiency of the school'. Rational decision-making processes are consistent with a search on the part of schools' managers for efficiency and effectiveness, but they are not the same as the attainment of efficiency, which is how they are treated in the *Handbook*. Much of what OFSTED treats as 'efficiency' would in standard usage be thought of as effectiveness. When the term 'effectiveness' is used in the *Handbook* it is often in the general sense of 'good practice'. The one item that comes near to the standard definition of effectiveness refers to planning the budget in relation to the school's educational objectives. But this is still an emphasis on process rather than on outcome. 'Effectiveness' in its public sector accounting sense is given little prominence in the *Framework* and is elided with efficiency.

The OFSTED definition of value for money

In principle, value for money is a highly significant concept for the education service as it focuses attention on how to get the best educational outcomes from a given expenditure of money. A crucial question, to which the answer has as yet proved elusive, is whether by spending more per pupil schools can achieve better educational outcomes. Currently in England there are considerable differences in the amount spent per pupil of the same age at schools of similar size, social composition and structure (in terms of sixth form provision and grant maintained status). In our sample of 66 schools there were otherwise similar schools with up to £400 difference in unit costs. A value for money judgement thus needs to balance an assessment of the quality of education provided against the resources available.

The 1993 version of the *Framework* gave inspectors only brief guidance on assessing value for money, stating that it is a judgement of the 'quality, standards, efficiency and effectiveness of the school in relation to the level of financial resources available to it' (OFSTED 1993d Part 2, p20). It would therefore appear that OFSTED expect inspectors to judge efficiency independently of the quantity of inputs, implying that efficiency is to be judged solely according to processes of decision-making. However a different interpretation is given in the *Guidance on the Inspection Schedule* which amplifies the evaluation criteria. Here efficiency is defined as an output–input relationship and is treated as equivalent to value for money.

> An efficient school makes the best use of all available resources to achieve high educational outcomes. In doing so it achieves value for money. (OFSTED 1993e Part 4, p11)

The OFSTED guidance does not distinguish at this point between efficiency and value for money since the definition of efficiency it offers is dependent upon inspectors making a value judgement, albeit based on sound evidence, about the quality or social value of the educational outputs of the school. The public sector accountancy definition of cost efficiency avoids this and leaves the value judgement about output to be reflected in the concept of effectiveness.

The required summative value for money judgement, however, relates output to input and is dependent on OFSTED's criteria for judging the quality of education. It requires inspectors to judge the effectiveness of the education provided by the school, 'after taking account of the context of the school and the achievement on entry of its pupils in relation to the 'money it uses''. The measure of resources available to the school focused upon in making the value for money judgement is the unit cost of the school. This is the total recurrent annual expenditure of the school divided by the number of pupils. It includes expenditure on staff, educational resources, premises and other costs. Thus the unit cost figure does not reflect differences in the value of schools' capital stock. It does, though, include expenditures funded out of the school's own income generation activities.

An attempt was made to offer further guidance on how to assess value for money in amendments to the OFSTED *Handbook* issued in May 1994. These included a table (Part 4, p84) which set out the order in which factors, all ranked on a 7 point scale, should be considered. Inspectors are advised first to consider their ranking of the pupils' socio-economic background and attainment on entry, then their judgement of standards and quality, followed by the efficiency of the school and ethos. Only at this stage is the unit cost considered and the summary value for money judgement reached. Far from clarifying the definition of value for money this advice in fact perpetuates and gives greater emphasis to confusion as to whether processes or outcomes are being assessed. An assessment of efficiency that takes no account of the quantity of inputs is highly idiosyncratic and inconsistent with other statements in the *Handbook*. Whereas the standard definition of value for money requires a comparison of effectiveness and efficiency, both input–output measures, OFSTED suggest that judgements about the quality of the educational process and the resource management process are compared to unit costs.

Inspectors' judgements on value for money

Given the problem of defining value for money in a way which can be meaningfully applied to schools, we examined the 66 inspection reports in order to assess how inspectors had attempted to reach value for money judgements and what factors appeared to influence these judgements.

Our data suggest that there are three categories of value for money judgement made by inspectors – good, satisfactory or fair, and unsatisfactory or not giving value. On this basis value for money was rated:

Good or very good	14 reports
Satisfactory or fair	31 reports
Unsatisfactory	5 reports
No summative value for money judgement	16 reports

The majority of value for money judgements are of the 'overall the school provides satisfactory value for money' nature. Only some provide further information of the thinking that lies behind the judgement. For example the following comment gives a view of unwise underspending.

> It was realised that the surplus (14% of available revenue funds) does not contribute best value for money for pupils currently at school. The Governing Body has, therefore agreed measures to reduce the surplus to a more efficient 4% within the current financial year. (OFSTED report)

Similarly there is evidence of criteria based judgement in another school where:

> The standards achieved in class, the extensive participation in extra-mural activities, the good results at GCSE level, and the excellent personal and social development of the pupils at a unit cost broadly in line with local costs, are all indications of the school providing good value for money. (OFSTED report)

There are reports where the effect of curricular arrangements are seen as detrimental to overall value.

> The school's commitment to a generously staffed PSE programme and its relatively small but wide ranging sixth form have displaced other priorities ... this has an adverse effect on the overall value for money. (OFSTED report)

However, the input–output relationship is revealed most clearly in the summative comment that:

> ... the school offers a generally satisfactory education at average costs and therefore provides sound value for money. (OFSTED report)

The balance between strategic decision-making and the efficient use of resources is summarised for one school as the need to:

> ... consider the implications of the balance between low contact ratio, higher

pupil teacher ratio, the low unit cost allocated to resources for learning and the amount held in contingency. (OFSTED report)

Of the seven schools with a contact ratio of over 80 per cent none are rated as giving good value for money, possibly reflecting wide acceptance of the view that 'the school may wish to consider the benefits of additional non-contact time for more staff'.

In some reports the inspectors' findings of ineffective processes for financial and resource management were crucial in leading to a poor value for money assessment rather than the quality of education. An example of such a judgement is:

> Given the poor level of financial control and decision making and the lack of accurate information and appropriate systems it is unlikely that the college is providing value for money. (OFSTED report)

However this is not always the case, indicating once more a degree of inconsistency in the reports. One school which has been highly praised in an investigation of effective management processes and is used as a model for others within the county has no judgement of value for money within the OFSTED report.

The nature of the value for money judgements

We also examined quantitative data culled from the reports to see what they might reveal about the factors associated with the value for money rating. We were interested to assess which of these factors appeared to influence inspectors in reaching their value for money judgement. The reports provide some summative quantitative indicators of effectiveness: one such indicator is the percentage of pupils gaining five or more GCSE passes at grades A to C. This can be contextualised against the percentage receiving free school meals. The other quantitative indicators of educational effectiveness are the percentage of lessons in which the quality of learning and the quality of teaching are graded as good, or as satisfactory and better. Indicators of resource inputs, such as unit cost and pupil–teacher ratio are also provided. For all their inadequacies these data provide the best nation wide information on school inputs and outputs yet assembled. Table 8.1 shows those indicators which we found more useful than the others in explaining what influenced value for money judgements.

We undertook two types of analysis: a comparison of selected schools and a statistical analysis of the whole sample. For the first we selected five schools which fell into the three categories of good, satisfactory and

Table 8.1 Performance indicators in school inspection reports

School Indicator	Form of Measurement	Variable Name
Social background of pupils	Percentage of pupils taking free school meals	FMEALS
Unit cost	Total recurrent annual budget of school (including funds raised by the school) divided by the number of pupils	UNITCOST
GCSE results	Percentage of pupils in age cohort gaining 5 or more grade A to C passes at GCSE	A–C5GCSE
A level	Average 'Advanced' level GCE score of students taking the examination	ALEVEL
Quality of teaching good or excellent	Percentage of lessons inspected for which inspectors made this judgement	QUALTGD
Quality of teaching satisfactory or better	Ditto	QUALTSAT
Quality of learning good or excellent	Ditto	QUALLGD
Quality of learning satisfactory or better	Ditto	QUALTSAT

unsatisfactory value for money judgements. The data for the three groups of schools are shown in Table 8.2. Under the quality of value for money (VFM) is recorded a short summary of the key qualitative factor supporting the value for money judgement.

Within the first sample group there is one selective school but the percentage with more than 5 GCSE at grades A to C is about or above average. As one moves down the table from good to satisfactory and then unsatisfactory VFM, the group average for GCSE results falls, as does the quality of learning and teaching rating, while the percentage of free school meals rises. The average unit cost of the five good VFM schools are higher than those of the satisfactory VFM but the low VFM schools have higher unit costs on average. There is some indication in the good VFM group that inspectors offset higher unit costs in schools G2 and G5 against their higher free school meals percentage and relatively good GCSE results and learning/teaching quality. School U2 has the same free

Table 8.2 Relationship between value for money, social data, and educational quality

School	Quality of VFM	%Free meals	%>5 GCSE	Quality of learning	Quality of teaching	Unit cost £	Sixth form
	Good						
G1	'strategic management'	6.4	45.1	90/55	88/53	2,116	yes
G2	'achievement'	25.1	34.3	77/30	71/28	2,249	no
G3	'all aspects'	14.8	49.4	87/53	93/63	2,160	yes
G4	'efficient, effective'	2.3	95.0	91/52	93/53	1,873	yes
G5	'targeting resources'	20.2	34.4	86/47	82/47	2,491	yes
Group average		13.8	51.6	86/47	85/57	2,178	
	Satisfactory...but						
S1	'required resources'	4.4	48.6	87/43	85/47	1,949	yes
S2	'formula ineffective'	2.7	44.6	75/20	87/41	1,779	yes
S3	'monitor resource use'	2.4	50.0	83/40	97/40	1,922	yes
S4	'criteria and evaluation'	58.2	17.9	79/30	78/37	2,302	no
S5	'cost effectiveness'	12.1	40.9	83/32	75/29	2,386	lower
Group average		16.0	40.4	82/33	84/39	2,067	
	Unsatisfactory						
U1	'split site management'	3.7	51.9	81/31	73/32	2,209	yes
U2	'weak achievement'	25.1	12.8	72/28	69/23	2,004	no
U3	'low numbers'	14.1	20.8	65/20	70/30	2,749	yes
U4	'budget not controlled'	47.2	4.1	52/18	58/?	2,762	lower
U5†	'curriculum needs'	40.1	5.7	73/?	73/?	3.332	yes
Group average		26.0	19.0	69/?	69/?	2,446‡	yes

Note: In the quality of learning and teaching columns the first number is the percentage of lessons graded 'satisfactory or better', and the second number is the percentage graded 'good or excellent'.

†U5 is a community school. The high unit cost would appear to include the additional funding for this. Unit cost as budget share per pupil is £2,508.

‡ Assumes unit cost for U5 is £2,508.

meals percentage as G2, lower unit cost and only slightly worse teaching and learning quality. However its GCSE results are very much lower, suggesting that it is this factor that puts it in the unsatisfactory category. It would also appear in the cases of S4 and S5 which have relatively high unit costs, that good GCSE results in relation to free meals percentage and reasonable quality ratings gives them a satisfactory VFM judgement compared to U3, U4 and U5 which can be matched for free school meals but have relatively worse GCSE results and lower quality ratings.

However it does not always appear to be the case that inspectors have balanced good exam results in relation to the social context and good quality ratings against higher unit cost in making their VFM judgement. For instance schools S1 and G1 have similar free school meals percentages and GCSE results but the unit cost of S1 are £167 less while its teaching and learning quality is only slightly lower. Another apparent inconsistency is the comparison of U1 and G2. U1 has lower unit costs and better teaching and learning quality and its exam results seem satisfactory given its free meals percentage. Yet the inspectors' judgement about the inefficiency of split site management appear to have been a major factor in the poor VFM judgement.

For our second method of analysis we investigated what factors were statistically significant in differentiating between good, satisfactory and poor value for money schools. Analysis of variance (ANOVA) tests were done to establish whether the average values of the performance, contextual and input variables were different between the three VFM groups of schools. The results of the ANOVA tests are reported in Table 8.3.

Table 8.3 One way analysis of variance tests on schools categorised by value for money

	VFM good	VFM satisfactory	VFM poor	F ratio	F probability <0.05 is significant
VARIABLE	Mean value	Mean value	Mean value		
QUALTGD	48.6%	40.5%	33.0%	4.13	0.0239
QUALTSAT	81.9%	82.7%	71.4%	3.02	0.0591
QUALLGD	48.5%	36%	31.3%	5.2	0.0100
QUALLSAT	87%	82%	73.8%	4.71	0.0142
A–C5GCSE	52.7%	39.5%	20.14%	4.79	0.0131
ALEVEL	14.1	11.5	11.9	1.12	0.3392
FMEAL	15%	18.2%	27.3%	1.11	0.3379
UNIT COST	£2,083	£2,099	£2,631	7.54	0.0015

Allocative efficiency is a fundamental theoretical concept in economics. It involves assumptions about the social value of what is produced and consumed and this in turn requires value judgements about income distribution

Only the quality of teaching and learning variables, GCSE results and unit cost have significantly different means for the three value for money groups. However the significance of differences in unit cost is only attributable to the much higher mean unit costs of the poor value for money schools. There is no significant difference between the unit cost means of the good and satisfactory value for money groups. It would appear that social disadvantage as measured by the percentage of pupils on free school meals is not significantly different between the three groups of schools despite the average percentage for poor VFM schools being considerably higher than for the other two categories. It must be borne in mind that the standard error for the poor VFM group is large because of the smallness of the sample (5 schools).

Further tests using discriminant analysis, which tests how well specific variables can predict which VFM group a school is placed in, were performed. However the only variables which had a significant F ratio were the proportion of lessons in which the quality of learning was good or excellent (QUALLGD) and the proportion in which teaching was good or excellent (QUALTGD). The other variables which were significant in one-way ANOVA tests were no longer so. This suggests that examination results and unit costs did not influence inspectors' judgements about value for money and that the percentage of learning and teaching assessed as satisfactory or better is not sufficient to discriminate between schools on VFM, whereas the percentage assessed as good or excellent is.

Conclusions

The statistical analysis of value for money judgements in relation to school performance indicators, while limited because of the small size of the sample, indicates that so far inspectors' judgements have been primarily influenced by their assessment of the quality of learning and teaching rather than by raw examination data or unit costs. However, with so few schools with poor value for money in our sample, it is not yet possible to reject the hypothesis that poor value for money schools are characterised by a high proportion of socially disadvantaged pupils. An indication that this might be the case, is the negative association we found between the percentage of pupils on free school meals and the quality of teaching and learning. In multiple regressions of the quality of teaching and learning as dependent variables, free school meals is the only significant independent variable, and has a negative coefficient, though the adjusted correlation coefficient is low. As unit costs are positively associated with the percentage of pupils on free school meals, since this is a factor attracting additional funding, it is more difficult for such schools to demonstrate good value for money.

We conclude from our examination of the VFM judgements that most are an attempt, as in the OFSTED guidance, to relate educational outcomes, after allowing for the social context, to monetary value of resources used. However it is not always apparent that this is how the VFM judgement has been reached and in some cases it would appear that the VFM judgement rests more on the inspectors' assessment of efficiency in relation to the processes of financial management. This finding relates back to our main theme that the conceptual framework is insufficiently clear because the concept of efficiency used by OFSTED relates to processes while the VFM judgement is intended as an output–input comparison. The lack of sufficiently clear guidance on the application of the value for money criteria leads to inconsistencies in the summative judgements and, in these early inspections, to omitting to make a value for money judgement at all. Given the difficulty of weighing up the different factors so that different inspection teams can reach consistent VFM judgements, we feel some concern that the value for money judgement is too crude to be useful.

Recommendations

It would assist in enhancing the consistency of inspectors' efficiency evaluations, the quality of their judgements and hence the impact of these in improving resource management practice if the conceptual basis of the efficiency criteria were made explicit and the evaluative criteria themselves made more consistent both within the OFSTED framework and in relation to standard definitions of the concepts of efficiency, effectiveness and value for money. A more extensive report on inspectors' assessment of management practice, supporting these recommendations, is provided by Levačić and Glover (1994).

The *Framework for Inspection* should make explicit the distinction between two strands in the evaluation criteria for efficiency. The output–input indicators of efficiency should be clearly distinguished from the process indicators of rational resource management. If the *Framework* referred to 'efficiency processes' rather than just 'efficiency' then it would not be offering conflicting definitions of efficiency as being both different from and identical to value for money. It would be consistent with the general usage of these concepts if inspectors made their judgement of the standards and quality of education in relation to the contextual factors and called this the effectiveness of the school. If a summary value for money judgement has to be made then it should be done by comparing the effectiveness of the school against its unit cost. The efficiency of the school, assessed in relation to process criteria should appear as a separate judgement on 'efficiency processes' since it is inappropriate to compare a process to the unit cost of production. It is therefore recommended that the *Framework* should make clear distinctions between the various evaluative criteria for 'the efficiency of the school' and separate out judgements about:

– processes
– the quality of inputs
– value for money as a summary comparison of school educational effectiveness against unit cost.

CHAPTER NINE

An Analysis of School Inspection Reports

by Jean Northam

By September 1993, OFSTED had published its first hundred inspection reports. These were undertaken by HMI and OFSTED Registered and team inspectors from March to July 1993. The succinct, clearly structured style was new, and their publication and ready availability was an important part of the openness and accountability of the new arrangements for inspections. An analysis of OFSTED's first hundred reports was carried out during the Autumn of 1993, to identify the major issues of concern to senior managers of schools. Between January and July 1994, a further 300 reports were analysed with particular reference to the assessment of schools at various levels, and the subjects of the curriculum. The detailed findings were made available to schools in the form of Walpole House Occasional Papers (Northam 1993, 1994a, 1994b).

No additional information was available about either the schools or the inspections. The purposes of the research were to discover how OFSTED's *Handbook for the Inspection of Schools* (OFSTED 1993c) had been applied in practice, and identify the priorities which had emerged from the detailed guidelines. It was hoped that the findings would assist school review, and give a flavour of the style, tone and vocabulary of the reports.

Major issues

Certain issues were raised in the great majority of reports across the spectrum of standards of performance, providing successful schools with guidelines for further development and weaker schools with priorities for urgent improvement. Extracts from reports are given to illustrate these issues.

Whole-school planning

A more systematic approach to whole-school planning, monitoring and review was required in most schools. The school's aims were not always specified in a form that would give clear guidance for planning and policy making, particularly in the longer term. In some cases, the aims and direction of school development needed to be more widely known and shared by staff, pupils and parents. Many inspectors emphasised the need for plans to be costed and set against a time scale. Financial planning often needed to be more clearly prioritised and linked more closely to priorities identified in the School Development Plan. In particular, arrangements for review were insufficiently developed, and there was insufficient staff involvement in planning and review in all but a small minority of the schools.

> The School Development Plan should specify the means by which progress can be reviewed and maintained. (Primary)

> The school's governing body, senior management and other staff should consider the need to identify priorities for development more systematically. (Secondary)

Staff roles and responsibilities

The issue of staff roles and responsibilities was frequently raised, especially where these were undefined or unclear or, as in the case of some secondary schools, variable from one department to another. Inspectors highlighted the urgent need for clearer role descriptions.

> All the teachers have job descriptions but for most their assigned roles are too limited to enable them to meet their responsibilities fully. (Primary)

> Senior and middle managers in the school need job descriptions which clearly define their responsibilities and set priorities. There needs to be a genuine delegation of authority and accountability. (Secondary)

There was a widespread need for the development of a co-ordinated whole-school structure of responsibilities – to improve consistency, cohesion and standards across the curriculum, and to provide a framework for curricular planning, organisation and review. The assessment, recording and reporting of pupils' progress could also vary from subject to subject or teacher to teacher, largely owing to the absence of agreed policies and guidelines. The information gained through assessment tended to be neglected in planning future work for pupils.

> The headteacher and staff should ensure that assessment becomes integral to teaching and learning and is reflected in both the long and short-term planning and in the organisation of the children. (Primary)

> The governors and head need ... to ensure that the staff plan and work more closely as a team. (Primary)

> The governors and senior management team should establish a forum for curricular debate and planning and carrying out a review of the curriculum as a whole in order to eliminate overlap and incorporate cross-subject components. (Secondary)

> Consistency of practice needs to be developed across departments in matters such as schemes of work, marking, reporting to parents and approaches to teaching and learning. (Secondary)

Curriculum co-ordination was a problem in a majority of primary schools, included in the Key Issues section of 59 per cent of the reports. In many schools, while other aspects of management were sound, organisational support for curriculum leaders was inadequate so that they lacked the necessary authority and arrangements for the development of their subject across the school.

> The headteacher should review the present management structure to rationalise, clarify and strengthen the roles of co-ordinators. (Primary)

> Teachers with curricular oversight do not have sufficient authority or non-contact time to monitor and develop the work of their colleagues. (Primary)

Inconsistencies in standards

Inconsistencies in the standards of achievement within a school featured prominently in the reports. There was variation in standards across Year groups, subjects, and Key Stages. While just over 17 per cent of the primary schools tended to achieve higher standards in Key Stage 2, 46 per cent were generally stronger in Key Stage 1. The latter tendency was particularly marked in technology, science and geography, and marginally less pronounced in mathematics, history and religious education. The only subject in which the schools were generally stronger in Key Stage 2 was physical education. Among the secondary schools, there was a slight tendency for standards to be higher in Key Stage 4 than in Key Stage 3, particularly in science, history and music, the reverse trend being apparent in religious education. In some secondary schools, these and other variations in standards were to some extent associated with the deployment of specialist staff, resources and accommodation.

> There is a need to review the effects of generous staffing in Years 10–12, because of the high contact ratio and the large size of many groups in Years 7–9. (Secondary)

> Due to inconsistencies in the amount of time and attention given to subjects in different classes, balance is not always achieved. (Primary)

Standards and quality of teaching and learning could also vary widely within a school. Among the sources of this variation, inspectors cited teachers' lack of confidence in their subject knowledge, poor pupil behaviour, lack of co-ordinated support and guidelines for the curriculum, weaknesses in the provision and use of time and resources, too narrow a range of teaching strategies to fulfil the requirements of the National Curriculum, and lack of development of cross-curricular skills and knowledge. In the primary schools, there was sometimes an under-emphasis on planned and systematic exposition and the acquisition of knowledge and understanding, while in secondary schools pupils could be given limited opportunities for investigation, learning independently and challenging information. The matching of tasks to the differing abilities of pupils was a recurrent weakness, with particular reference to more able pupils or those with some difficulties in learning.

To support teachers in improving standards and quality, inspectors recommended a more systematic and closely targeted approach to staff development. School Development Plans often lacked thorough short and longer term planning for staff development, costed and prioritised in terms of the broader aims and objectives of the school. In some reports, special mention was made of part-time, non-specialist, supply and support staff, particularly where there was a lack of guidance for them or where their effectiveness was limited by their absence from the planning process.

> There were ... significant limitations in the range of teaching methods used and in the teachers' understanding of National Curriculum subjects. (Primary)
>
> In a minority of lessons the work is insufficiently matched to children's needs and abilities and the pupils become restless, inattentive and insufficiently motivated. (Primary)
>
> At present the School Development Plan does not adequately identify future needs ... plans for curriculum development should include aspects of resourcing and in-service provision. (Primary)
>
> Most of the SEN teachers lacked recent specialist INSET. (Secondary)
>
> More attention should be paid to the skills of information handling, such as skimming, scanning and note-taking. (Secondary)

Inspectors noted shortcomings in policy or practice regarding ethnic and gender differences, which were sometimes associated with variations in standards and quality of teaching and learning.

> The school needs to review the factors that influence pupils' (subject) choices ... (and) should also be aware of the pronounced gender imbalance of its staffing structure. (Secondary)
>
> At times the boys tend to dominate the playground space with games of football and in the poorly managed classes a high noise level disadvantages all the pupils. (Primary)

Assessments of school performance

The reports were analysed to identify major features of schools assessed at different levels. In the majority of reports, a statement of the general assessment was given at or near the beginning of the 'Main Findings' section. Some examples were: 'This is a successful school with many strengths'; 'this is a very good school'; 'overall standards in this school are unsatisfactory in most subjects'.

Without inside knowledge of the inspection process, the researcher needed to rely solely on the inspection reports made public by OFSTED to gauge the standard achieved by the schools. In this respect the researcher was in the same position as parents, press and public. The vocabulary used to describe the categories of assessment is taken from the reports rather than the official guidance as, again, this is in line with the information presented to parents.

Good and successful schools

Almost 30 per cent of the secondary schools fell into this category, of which 7 per cent were described as 'very good', and 13 per cent of the primary schools. The good schools shared the following features:

- Clear school aims and a strong ethos, understood and shared by the whole school community.
- Headship strong in management ability, leadership and vision.
- Close co-operation between head teacher and governors.
- Staff conscientious and strongly committed to the school.
- A management style encouraging staff participation in decision-making.
- Good, mutually respectful relationships among and between adults and pupils.
- Good pupil behaviour with opportunities to assume roles of responsibility.
- High levels of pupil motivation.
- Clear, well-monitored routines regulating the school day.
- Standards and quality in teaching and learning good in most lessons and never weak.
- Good results in public examinations, relative to the ability range among the pupils.
- Good provision for pupils' social, cultural, spiritual and moral development, and for pastoral support.
- Good provision for pupils with special educational needs.
- A broad and balanced curriculum.
- Close involvement of parents and governors in the life of the school.

- A well-presented environment.
- Strong support from and links with the community.

Most schools described as 'good' or 'successful' admitted pupils who were socially neither advantaged or disadvantaged, though about 10 per cent of 'good' secondary schools had an ability range skewed towards the less able, and 20 per cent towards the more able.

Among schools described as 'very good', none of which were primary, 40 per cent were selective and a similar proportion were single sex schools. While the majority admitted relatively advantaged pupils, 30 per cent had a school population skewed towards less able or disadvantaged pupils. All these schools reported a low incidence of exclusion and unauthorised absence, and most were highly popular, with rising rolls.

Reports on the schools in this category adopted a highly favourable tone, and the 'Main Findings' sections summarised what the inspectors would expect to find in a good school, for example:

> (Name) is a good school with a friendly, hardworking and civilised atmosphere. Most of its pupils achieve consistently well in relation to their ages and abilities .... The school provides a well-planned and largely balanced curriculum, enriched by an impressive array of extra-curricular activities, which contribute much to the cultural and social development of the pupils. Pupils are given every encouragement to develop their spiritual and moral values ... The good qualities of the school are due in no small measure to the presence of a well-qualified and dedicated teaching staff, well-supported by capable and committed support staff, and led with intelligence, efficiency and enterprise. (Secondary)

Satisfactory with strengths

About a third of the secondary and 12 per cent of the primary schools came into this category. While they shared many of the features of 'good' schools, the proportion of lessons in which standards and quality were good was either lower or balanced by pockets of unsatisfactory work. Inspectors used a number of phrases to indicate that the school was more than satisfactory, but not yet quite good enough to achieve the highest grading.

> (Name) has many of the features of a successful school.

> Standards of achievement in lessons are, on the whole, satisfactory or better and there are specific subjects in which these standards are high .... The quality of learning is good ... with some good teaching in nearly all departments ... but there is poor teaching in a number of departments. (Secondary)

There was usually some urgency about one or more of the Key Issues to be addressed by the school, concerning overall management and policy making, standards in at least one subject or among a group of pupils, or the suitability and safety of accommodation and resources.

> The school needs clearer aims in order to give common purpose to management and to strategies for the whole school ... (Secondary)

> Action is required regarding aspects of security, maintenance, decor and cleaning .... In science there is inappropriate storage of flammables and corrosives ... (Secondary)

> (Governors and SMT should take action to address) ... the underachievement of boys ... (Secondary)

> The provision for art should be reviewed and that for religious education urgently reviewed to raise standards in these subjects. (Primary)

> The governors and senior management team should give attention to ... the development of a whole school curriculum framework ... (Primary)

> The headteacher and staff should ensure that the organisation of the reception class provides security and sustained periods of teaching and learning. (Primary)

Generally satisfactory

In just over a quarter of the secondary schools, inspectors found that standards were sound or satisfactory, on the whole, but with some unevenness. There were shortcomings in policies and procedures in the great majority. Management systems were often insufficiently developed to improve consistency and share good practice, and lines of accountability and responsibility were sometimes unclear. The most frequently mentioned criticism was that longer term planning was lacking, including clear statements of the aims of the school, and the School Development Plan tended to be inadequate in some respects. The school curriculum was often in need of review, and teachers needed to be supported in a concerted effort to bring all teaching up to the standard of the best practice in the school. In many of these schools, there were deficiencies in the school environment and in curriculum resources.

> The school development plan needs to focus on fewer issues. There needs to be a more precisely defined time scale ... (Secondary)

> Senior and middle managers should review the planning, teaching and assessment of the National Curriculum. (Secondary)

> Urgent attention must be paid to improving the amount and quality of specialist science accommodation. (Secondary)

> The aims and objectives need reconsideration if a clear sense of direction is to be provided. (Secondary)

Well over half the primary schools had a report which indicated that they were generally satisfactory, though the opening statements of many were so complex and hedged with reservations that it was difficult to discern the overall assessment. It is possible that the inspection teams considered some of these schools to be less than satisfactory, but had not included an unequivocal statement to that effect.

The weaknesses among these primary schools were similar to those in the 'generally satisfactory' secondary schools. There was some variability within subjects, often reflecting weaknesses in curriculum co-ordination and schemes of work, and teachers' lack of confidence in their subject knowledge. The allocation of time to subjects was a recurring issue. Some schools had problems with financial management and administration.

> The teaching time allocated to Key Stage 2 is substantially below the recommended level. (Primary)

> There were significant limitations in the range of teaching methods used and in the teachers' understanding of National Curriculum subjects. (Primary)

> In English, standards in reading, speaking and listening are satisfactory, but unsatisfactory in writing, handwriting and spelling. (Primary)

> There is no clear whole school framework to ensure balance and continuity. (Primary)

> Procedures for setting and monitoring the budget are unsatisfactory. (Primary)

The 'generally satisfactory' schools had strengths as well as weaknesses, frequently maintaining good relationships, positive attitudes and ethos, and a high standard of pastoral care.

Standards varying from satisfactory to unsatisfactory

In almost 10 per cent of secondary and primary schools, standards were satisfactory in at least 60 per cent of lessons, and in most subjects, but in other subjects fell significantly below the level that could reasonably be expected of the pupils. There were weaknesses in management and in the curriculum, and support and in-service provision for the staff were needed urgently. Teachers' subject knowledge, and non-specialist teaching at secondary level, were issues for many of these schools.

> The School Development Plan should present a clear plan of action ... (Primary)

> Underachievement is noted in several areas of the curriculum particularly amongst boys and the relatively few abler pupils. (Secondary)

> Teachers are insufficiently supported when teaching in curriculum areas for which they have no formal qualifications. (Secondary)

Four-fifths of these secondary schools admitted an intake which was skewed towards less able pupils or those from areas of social and economic disadvantage. Some pupils at certain of these schools had been excluded from other schools in the area. Falling rolls caused problems for many of them, with attendant funding and staffing difficulties. There was some evidence that the transition from primary school might have had particular importance for some of these schools, where, for example, pupils' performance declined from Year 6 to Year 7, or where patterns of unauthorised absence, sometimes associated with family difficulties, had their origins in the primary school and had become firmly established after transfer to secondary school.

Overall standards generally unsatisfactory

Four per cent of the primary schools were assessed as unsatisfactory, and a further 5 per cent were a cause for serious concern. Among the secondary schools, the proportions were less than 2 per cent. Dull teaching, lack of challenge, and poor pupil behaviour contributed to low standards and poor quality of teaching and learning in a significant proportion of lessons. Time in some lessons was wasted and poorly managed. Standards were often unacceptably low in schools which were causing serious concern, and were satisfactory in fewer than 50 per cent of the lessons.

> Poor behaviour is the most significant obstacle to effective learning. In too many lessons pupils are required to carry out simple tasks such as copying texts or colouring diagrams.

> Some pupils have very low self-esteem and do not consider themselves to be capable of achieving much. More needs to be done to dispel this belief and challenge pupils with fulfilling work.

There were weaknesses in management in many of these schools, though some had newly appointed head teachers whose efforts to improve the school were acknowledged and endorsed by the inspection team.

> The school is not yet fully efficient or effective ...

> The financial management is poor ...

> Under the new headteacher, a start has been made on enabling staff to co-operate more closely.

Profile of the good school

While reports varied in quality, many were detailed and penetrating in their analysis of the sources of strength and weakness in schools. The research into a large sample of reports yielded a wealth of information on all areas of equal school life, making it possible to compile a check-list of features of a hypothetical 'good school'. The following check-list, quoted from OFSTED's First Hundred (Northam 1993), is a compilation of recommendations for improving teaching and learning.

Teaching and learning in the good school

1. In all subjects pupils can:
   - show basic competence in numeracy and literacy
   - read aloud with confidence
   - show confidence in oral work
   - converse and discuss readily
   - demonstrate initiative
   - develop an argument in depth
   - pose questions
   - solve problems
   - show skill in investigation and research
   - seek information from books and other sources
   - learn independently
   - write for different purposes and audiences
   - draft and redraft written work
   - apply prior learning
   - apply numerical and graphical skills
   - understand and pursue the purpose of the lesson
   - evaluate the work of self and others.

2. Across the curriculum teachers can:
   - differentiate work for different pupils
   - match levels of work to the abilities of pupils
   - use a variety of teaching approaches
   - provide for individuals, groups and whole classes
   - make appropriate use of Information Technology
   - provide sufficient challenge for the most able
   - provide for children with special educational needs
   - set purposeful, planned homework
   - foster initiative and independent learning
   - encourage active participation in lessons
   - respond to pupils' efforts with praise and support
   - develop pupils' numeracy, literacy and oracy
   - develop pupils' technological and investigative skills.

3. Policy on Assessment, Recording and Reporting includes:
   - criteria for grades or marks
   - guidance on standards of marking
   - advice on writing explanatory comments on pupils' work
   - accessibility of records
   - records of achievement and pupil self-evaluation
   - provision for the follow-up of tests and assessments
   - good provision for reporting to parents
   - use of assessment information in planning

– a co-ordinated and consistent whole-school approach to assessment
– recording and reporting.

Concluding comments

While the tone of the reports was impersonal and precise, bordering at times on the pedantic, the reporting was also capable of subtleties and colour, suggesting, for example, enthusiasm or sympathetic understanding. Inspectors sometimes make the point that 'satisfactory' is not a synonym for 'nondescript': this is borne out in the reports which included observations and examples to illustrate the distinctive nature of each school. The impression given by the reports was that the inspectors recognised the importance of high morale among the staff, and how readily this might be damaged by unbalanced reporting on their work.

Part Four: The Schools' Perspective

CHAPTER TEN

Schools' Experiences of Inspection

by Sheila Russell

In September 1992 the first training courses for independent inspectors were held, the OFSTED logo was unveiled and participants were sold the newly published *Handbook for the Inspection of Schools*. Since my introduction in that week I have led inspections of primary and secondary schools as a Registered Inspector, and worked as a consultant to support schools' preparation for inspection and for action afterwards. Through these different experiences, standing in different relationships to schools, I began to form my view of how schools experience inspection in practice. Nevertheless in these roles my perceptions have necessarily been limited by the extent to which people felt they could be frank and open with me about their hopes and fears.

In 1994, at Leeds Metropolitan University, we began a research project to investigate the relationship between school inspection and the professional development of individual teachers, and we interviewed over 30 teachers and head teachers from six different schools inspected in 1994. In group interviews in September 1994 we validated our early findings against the experiences of other schools, and we are continuing our investigation through action research in three schools as they work on improvement post-inspection.

It is the information from this study that has proved most illuminating and thought-provoking in forming my views on the effects of inspection on schools, and the ideas in this chapter derive directly from what teachers and head teachers have told us.

Inspection and improvement

We found that those who work in schools have different perceptions from inspectors about the real purpose of inspection. The official line is concisely stated by OFSTED as 'Improvement through Inspection', and is expanded in this way: 'The central purpose of the report is to identify the strengths and weaknesses of a school, the overall quality of education provided, the standards pupils are achieving, and what should be done if improvements are needed' (OFSTED 1994h, *Guidance on the Inspection Schedule*, p22).

OFSTED's model makes the process of school improvement look considerably less problematic than we all know it to be in practice. It supposes that a secure and valid judgement is made about the school by independent outsiders; that issues where action is needed are highlighted; that there is clear communication of these findings to those responsible and that they then fulfil their obligations by writing an action plan to bring about the needed improvements. As the official circular states:

> The governing body will need to make consideration of the report and its findings an urgent priority, as it is obliged to draw up and publish an action plan setting out specific action to be taken in response to the report and the timetable on which it will be carried out. (DFE 1993)

The problematic nature of bringing about effective change in schools has been a matter of concern for many writers and researchers over recent years and their conclusions throw light on the likely success of the OFSTED model. Hargreaves and Hopkins (1991, p106) summarise some of the necessary conditions for successful school improvement, in particular in relation to the existence and interaction of external and internal pressure and support. There should be some external support as part of a strategic partnership (e.g. with INSET providers and LEA advisers). However without external pressure (e.g. an inspection, or expressions of parental dissatisfaction) a school may not move from 'its stable pattern of self-maintenance'. External pressure must be linked to internal pressure, coming from a recognition by governors, head and senior staff of the advantages of any new development to the school itself. Conditions like this can lead to 'internal support', a release of self-help and self-directing energy. Describing successful initiatives for change, Hopkins, Ainscow and West (1994, p82) judge that 'on all the evidence so far, this appears to be the only form of partnership which can help those schools which are underperforming to become more successful'.

The OFSTED model recognises the importance of external support, and indeed the *Framework for the Inspection of Schools* has been seen by many as part of that support and guidance. The external pressure is also certainly there (excessively so, some would say). In this chapter I want to examine how effectively OFSTED inspection creates the other two conditions, the necessary internal pressure and internal support for effective change. The framework for school improvement described by Hopkins, Ainscow and West (p103) stresses the importance of identifying, creating, and working on the internal conditions in a school that sustain and manage change. The effect of inspection can slow down this essential work.

Schools' expectations of inspection

Many teachers doubt that the 'identification of strengths and weaknesses' is genuinely intended to be helpful. Inspections often start off with a degree of mistrust, and the implications of this are sometimes overlooked by inspectors and by OFSTED. One head told us: '(the staff) feel that the inspectors aren't coming to see the positives, they are coming to look for the negatives, and no matter what I say this is what they feel'; another that 'I get the distinct impression that the Government's idea behind this was that we are going to show up that a very large majority of schools in this country are not doing a good job' and another that 'the agenda is to find out what is wrong and that is a very disruptive process particularly in terms of teacher morale'.

One consequence of these perceptions is that many teachers talk of inspection in terms of 'them' coming to do something to 'us'. In relation to OFSTED, teachers from different schools ask each other 'Have you been done yet?' Despite Registered Inspectors meeting staff beforehand to explain the process, as recommended by OFSTED, there is still strong evidence of concern about what Wragg (1995, p64) described as 'the disruption to the school's working life; the gibberish of the final report; the feeling of having being done over, however skilfully; the lack of follow-up, continuity and aftercare'.

In addition there are very real fears about the effect of a poor, or even relatively poor, report on the likelihood of a school being selected for closure or an individual teacher being selected for redundancy. Although it could be argued that selection for redundancy should not be on the basis of performance, we know of instances of governing bodies asking inspection teams to identify weak teachers, so such concerns are not excessive or paranoid.

One head of department reported:

'In a case like our town with its one secondary school too many, a bad OFSTED report could mean the closure of that school ... we had our prize giving last night and the head master said that, if our school report had been bad it could have had disastrous effects on the school, because there's about 700 surplus places in the town':

and at a more personal level teachers told us: 'we are all concerned big brother is going to sack us', and from the same school:

> 'If they gave me a million pounds I couldn't work any harder than I do and it's as simple as that. So if I'm not good enough then they can sack me because I think I am, I think I'm all right.'

For these sorts of reasons, and because teaching is already a difficult and demanding job, there is a high level of anxiety and stress associated with inspection. Our series of interviews was with secondary and middle school teachers but we have seen this just as much, if not more, in the past year amongst primary school teachers.

It was not uncommon for teachers to tell us of anxiety and insomnia; this deputy head was typical: 'to be honest I go to sleep thinking about it and I wake up thinking about it'.

At best the inspection situation is seen as artificial and unnatural, a test to be survived. A teacher in a middle school told us: 'It's a very daunting task that the whole feeling of the school for a whole week is 'You've got to be perfect'.'

When the preparation for a collaborative effort to survive an inspection takes up so much energy it is perhaps not surprising that one teacher said: 'Now I didn't even know about that piece of paper, you know, the action plan thing' and others, heads included, told us that they had not thought beyond the inspection week itself in their preparation.

The danger with a simplistic application of the OFSTED model for improvement is that it can ignore the effect of this climate of anxiety and concern amongst teachers. This climate, and the expectations we found when we interviewed teachers before and after inspection inhibited the 'release of self-directing energy' as a support for improvement. We did discover that, once teachers had found their own ways to survive the inspection upheaval (trauma would not be an inappropriate word), there could be a regeneration of energy in the school, and the necessary internal pressure for change. However, to get the most out of inspection, managers and inspectors cannot afford to ignore the emotions which are present alongside the logic of the inspection model.

Relations with inspectors

Many teachers recalled an atmosphere in the week of the inspection that was based on cautious mutual respect between teachers and inspectors. Some told us of their hope that the inspectors' wide experience of observing practice in a number of schools would enable them to give an overview of the school in a better way than an insider. Despite the initial misgivings of teachers, inspection teams often convinced them of their knowledge and sensitivity. In general teachers found the week of the inspection to be less bad than they had feared. One union representative, referring to his suspicions of the motives behind inspection, told us '... with this sort of history I think it is quite remarkable that relations between schools and inspecting teams are as good as they are, to be honest'.

However to create the 'internal pressure' that derives from a belief that required changes are central to a school's development there has to be more than this; there has to be a real understanding and acceptance of the inspectors' message and findings. There are various features of inspection that make this acceptance more, or less likely.

Teachers preferred inspectors who were approachable and who did not fit the stereotype of unsmiling bureaucrats in grey suits. Nevertheless affability did not lead automatically to trust, and as one teacher pointed out: 'I felt they were quite convivial. I didn't trust them, but they were nice. I was very wary of what was said'. And this wariness was echoed by another: 'They were very pleasant people, but having said that I imagine they were probably trained to be very pleasant, I don't know, trained to be pleasant and find things out.'

Some schools turned the tables on the inspectors and operated a system of inspecting the inspectors. One school is even marketing its *Inspection Monitoring Framework* to other schools. Certainly this reaction puts the inspectors themselves under pressure and may even act as an additional barrier to effective communication.

Messages and feedback

The majority of teachers value direct feedback from the inspectors about the lessons observed. This was highlighted in the Coopers & Lybrand (1994, p26) review of the first 100 OFSTED inspections: 'In over half the schools, staff were disappointed that there was not more opportunity for discussion with inspectors after lessons'.

The evidence does suggest that the greater the extent of professional dialogue between individual teachers and inspectors the more ready teachers will be to take seriously the findings and recommendations that are made. This is also the case in relation to the more formal oral feedback which, at subject level in secondary schools, is usually delivered by inspectors to heads of departments, with a senior member of staff in attendance. In some cases this formal feedback has been preceded by an informal discussion with a greater emphasis on professional dialogue. One teacher told us:

'If the lady left at the end of the week not having written a report even the conversations that she'd had with me would have been quite valuable in backing up my own feelings'.

A head teacher also highlighted this as a positive feature of an inspection:

'Now this is where I think the discussions with the head of department and the inspector were important, because as I've said our inspectors did sit down with the heads of departments and said, 'Look, this isn't in the report, but this is what we think', and that, I think, had a far greater influence on the heads of departments because they went away and talked with their departmental staff .... We had the heads of departments' meeting and they were very open about what had actually been said to them by the inspectors and what their departments ought to have or not to have been doing.'

Another head from a school inspected very early on in the system told me that it took her staff nearly six months to begin any effective action on the inspection findings, and then that was principally based on the conversations they had valued with subject inspectors; the report itself was 'too bland'.

For some the formal feedback was seen variously as too impersonal or too rushed. Sometimes too little time is offered for reflection, and notes taken hastily can give an unbalanced view. There is a tendency to write down the negatives and the 'points for action' and this distorted feedback then gets passed on by the head of department to his or her colleagues. The head of department can feel quite bewildered too, as one said:

'At the end of it you get so bamboozled by all these words, above average, satisfactory, good, all these words coming out, and at the end of that lot you think 'I don't know what he's just said' .... And I said 'was it all right then?' and he went 'yes, fine'.'

The possible confusion about the message indicates that feedback should be given directly to as many people as possible. The same head of department went on to say:

'I felt very sorry for all the members of my department who have been leading up to this week, getting themselves upset about it and doing their best during the week we had these inspectors in, all of a sudden on the Wednesday night I think it was, I had this feedback and in a way I felt quite relieved and quite elated about the whole thing. These people haven't got any of this feedback and so the whole week in a way just went like that for them, it just fell flat and they did not actually get an inspector to talk to or to feed back to or to discuss anything at all with them.'

Wilcox (1992) characterises features of evaluation which lead to trustworthy conclusions and refers to the importance of 'member checks' where the interpretations and conclusions of an evaluation can be tested with members of the groups from whom the data were collected. This process is not essentially present in school inspection, and some teams of inspectors regard it as inappropriate. Our conversations with teachers indicate that an absence of this approach makes the final conclusions less likely to lead to successful action for change. As one head teacher said: 'There's a chance you could risk the improvement for the want of looking at the most effective way of giving people feedback.'

Approaches to action planning

Often it is the oral feedback that gives the clearest message. As we have seen, the written conclusions sometimes seem 'bland' or, as Wragg puts it more forcibly, 'gibberish'. This may be because of the inherent complexity of defining precise strategies that will improve schools, or because the climate of anxiety inhibits inspectors from being too direct in suggesting any action. Whatever the reason we find that the 'Key Issues' identified by inspectors contain phrases such as 'build on the progress ... by increased monitoring ...'; 'continue to define, implement and evaluate ... '; 'review and extend the teaching strategies ...'.

Faced with these recommendations a school may respond in its action plan by appearing to go back to the beginning. After a full school inspection, and a complete report on the quality of teaching and learning, how are we to explain the fact that action plans often start with the task of 'reviewing', and then continue to 'identify areas of good practice'? Despite all the work that has gone into inspection and reporting, it seems that the only way to reach the 'internal pressure' and, most importantly, the energy of 'internal support' is for at least some of the evaluative work to be carried out again in the school.

Table 10.1 sets out five issues for five different schools, as they were presented in the inspectors' reports. In column 2 of the table there are some extracts from the reports themselves, which show why the issues were considered to be significant. In column 3 there is a summary of some of the action points set out by the schools, and made public by their governing bodies.

While not all of the actions proposed have the effect of taking the school back to the start of a reviewing process, there are many examples of strategies such as those quoted in the table, which imply that observation and discussion must precede any identification of specific changes.

Wilcox and Gray (1994, p257) describe inspections as potential learning experiences but emphasise that 'the learning is potential in the sense that teachers first have to be persuaded that the findings are 'true', then internalise them, and finally accept a share in collective responsibility for

Table 10.1 School Issues and Action

ISSUE	EXTRACT FROM REPORT	EXTRACT FROM ACTION PLAN
School A Take action to improve standards in Key Stage 3	There is significant underachievement by pupils generally. In over 40% of lessons at Key Stage 3 pupils were judged to be underachieving	Review present monitoring of progress. Identify areas of good practice leading to high achievement
School B Continue to define, implement and evaluate strategies to increase the numbers of pupils who gain A-C grades in GCSE examinations	Standards of achievement are low. The proportion of pupils gaining 5 or more A-C grades was significantly lower than the national average (14% in 1994, national average 43%)	Head to meet with heads of departments to review and analyse recent exam results. Issue to be a priority in the action plan of each department
School C Build on the recent progress in raising standards of achievement by increased monitoring of curriculum policy and of teaching and learning styles	The pupils would benefit from a wider range of teaching styles...more opportunities could be created for pupils to take responsibility for their own learning	Extra levels of monitoring...add to job descriptions...guidance on department policies...INSET on teaching and learning styles...classroom observation
School D Ensure that the whole staff take collective responsibility for the meeting of all pupils' needs through a range of teaching and learning strategies	Lessons are generally highly structured and do not always allow individuality and pupils to take responsibility for their own learning	Staff residential conference...whole school teaching and learning development strategy... observation of good practice...INSET on active learning
School E Review and extend the teaching strategies employed and the organisation of teaching groups so as to motivate lower achievers to make the best progress possible	Many young people arrive at the school not able to take full advantage of secondary education through lack of basic skills....They achieve quite well in comparison with their capabilities	INSET...classroom observation and support programmes supported by deputy heads and incorporated in Staff Appraisal scheme

doing something about them'. The response through published action plans seems to suggest that, at least for major issues of achievement and teaching methods, those planning at school level are reluctant to impose change that has not been thought through over a period of time by the staff involved.

But schools where standards of achievement (measured by the number of pupils gaining five A-C grades at GCSE) are low in comparison to the national average may not have time for a measured approach to action to bear fruit. For them the OFSTED visit to monitor the implementation of action may come too soon for any real change to be discerned. At worst this will lead to the school being described as in need of special measures, after it has already undergone some self-review and is beginning the slow process of change. Some will argue that, for the sake of pupils in these schools, OFSTED should not delay its monitoring visit. Yet there is little empirical evidence to show that standards can be more rapidly improved by a process that imposes action rather than one which generates ideas more collaboratively. However in the climate of fear and uncertainty schools may, pragmatically, adopt a more top-down approach, or even one where the action plan sets out superficial changes which they hope will keep the inspectors at bay for a while. Such tactics would run counter to the challenge issued to heads by Fullan (1992, p61) 'to improve education in the only way it can be – through the day-to-day actions of empowered individuals'.

Leadership and management

Under these pressures school leaders need to be resolute in their choice of strategy. We found that the effectiveness of the action after an inspection depends to a great extent on the quality of leadership in the school. Once the experience has been 'survived', as one head told us 'I would say there is a tremendous feeling of relief and there is a tremendous problem in remotivation.'

In one school the reaction was described in this way:

'After the pain of an inspection, you've got two alternatives, you can circle the wagons and keep 'em out, which does no good, or you say what can we get out of it ... we take it from the positive side and say 'how are we going to move forward'.'

Once they realise what is required next, most teachers make the best of things. A head of department from the same school commented:

'I do genuinely feel that the four or five areas we're working in we all knew needed attention, and I'm still positive that most of our staff are working in these areas, willingly might be a strong word, but they're doing it because they genuinely believe it needs doing.'

The structure of the report makes it difficult for schools to select a few priorities to work on in one year. Most managers would agree that four or five areas for whole school attention is too many, and can lead to the energy from good intentions being dissipated. Changes in the inspection framework in 1996 may help schools to deal with this by listing issues in an agreed order of priority.

In the long term one of the most influential effects of OFSTED inspections of secondary schools may turn out to be a clarification, perhaps even change, of the role of middle management. There are three principal effects. For some departments it started with the preparation, or revision, of schemes of work. One deputy head explained:

'They've all had a session, a half day at least, with their adviser to look through the documentation, and get everything sorted out within the department'

and a head of department commented of this process:

'I think most of the things I have been asked to do are things which I was either doing or should have done.'

The second effect is on the expectations of leadership and responsibility for action after inspection, from those in middle management roles. A head teacher described this change:

'They now feel a responsibility to manage, and in the action plan there's a management role for our heads of department in terms of their staff, the things that they can and should be doing with their staff now on a more formal and regular basis. I think that need to be open is what's created a different approach for many of the heads of departments, the fact that everything is there for everyone to see.'

The heads of department from other schools could see the value in this approach, as one said:

'If a head or SMT impose an action plan in response to the issues yes, that's a disaster, at least we were all given an input, we were told we would have to put an input into the action plan, and it was done on a departmental basis, and a whole school basis ... and therefore I suppose it has been much more useful from that point of view.'

The third change is often implicit in the phrasing of key issues from inspectors, which require 'monitoring and evaluation' of classroom activities. At secondary level this could be the most significant change, continuing the opening up of the activity of teaching that has begun through classroom observation in appraisal. It is still a very sensitive area, but the inspection has provided some models. For instance one school has built pupil tracking by heads of departments into its action plan, and they have discussed their perceptions of the experiences of pupils in a school day, and have used this knowledge to plan changes.

In primary schools a different model for management and leadership is required, and unless inspectors are very sensitive to the constraints of a full teaching day, the use of the inspection *Framework* can lead to a secondary model being applied inappropriately, and to the report making unrealistic allusions to the tasks of subject co-ordinators. In HMCI's Report (OFSTED 1995a, p6) the responsibility for curriculum leadership is placed firmly on the head teacher with this comment

'Relatively few headteachers, however, spend sufficient time evaluating the quality of teaching and learning. Many should play a stronger part in curriculum development.'

Can improvement be sustained internally through revised management responsibilities? Continued monitoring at school level may be sufficient, but even those schools most committed to their action had doubts:

'The reality is unless there is somebody regularly checking up on you, keeping an eye on you, helping you over the four years, schools may with the best will in the world drift.'

Improving the system

There is a recognition amongst teachers that the external pressure of inspection can be a necessary catalyst to make things happen:

'I think anybody in any job, and teachers are no exception, you need some kind of external stimulus to make you do something, and if somebody said to me now, you've got to go home tonight and redraft a scheme of work for year nine, I'd think 'Oh God' but if somebody said redraft a scheme for year nine because we have the inspectors arriving in three weeks' time I think well I'd probably show some interest in it then, and I think that's human.'

Having acknowledged that some pressure is needed, there is still considerable doubt expressed by teachers that the particular way of interacting with inspectors dictated by the OFSTED model is the most effective one:

'We said we would much rather have an inspector attached to our department for half a term, and who came in two half days a week or whatever, and he came as part of the department and was with us for a longer time, and then sat down constructively at the end of the time to plan a programme of development.'

In February 1995, after four terms of inspection, with monitoring and quality assurance checks by OFSTED which included seeking the views of those inspected, a new *Framework for the Inspection of Schools* was proposed (OFSTED 1995b). Some features of the new proposals acknowledge the inadvertent stress that has been caused to schools by the process of inspection, and are intended to 'lighten' this burden, particularly for smaller schools. There is an explicit intention to reduce the amount of documentation a school might be expected to provide, for instance. However by now the myth of what inspection means is so deeply embedded in teachers' culture that these changes may be slow to have a significant effect on reducing the upheaval of an inspection.

More important is the acknowledgement in the new proposals of the importance of the school's present priorities based on its own self-evaluation process. It is further suggested that schools should discuss, and agree the priority of, each of the key issues identified by inspectors. This change may lead to a deeper understanding and acceptance of the issues as really important for action at school level.

Our research indicates that there are further areas where the inspection process could be improved, which are not fully dealt with in the new proposals. Teachers would welcome a greater partnership with those evaluating them, incorporating more opportunity for discussion and feedback, and more involvement of the inspectors in their planning for action. For this to happen the culture of inspecting has to change, and realistic amounts of time given to those aspects of inspection believed by many to be most effective in bringing about that understanding of judgements needed for the internal dynamic of change.

Secondly the time-scale for action needs to be realistic. A good pace is important for change to be rewarding, and setting deadlines is undeniably an important way of sustaining motivation and ensuring that action is not superficial. However, monitoring by OFSTED at an early stage may not be the best form of external pressure to apply. Once inspections have taken place we need to examine carefully the most effective forms of external pressure and support for a changing school.

Conclusion

OFSTED inspection creates some of the external pressure believed to be necessary for a school to change, but at considerable financial and emotional cost. While a school's attention is focused on preparing for inspection there may be less time or resources for other activities. One head of a small primary school told me she could not afford to start to replace the school's mathematics scheme this year because the money would be needed for 'preparing for OFSTED'.

As inspectors have applied it, and schools have responded, the model places undue emphasis on the 'audit' stage of an improvement cycle. It is even more a matter of concern, then, that inspectors' issues often prompt schools to repeat the 'review' stage, before embarking on action. There is evidence both in inspectors' recommendations and in school action plan responses that the external view is not enough to prompt change, and that the internalisation of findings as school priorities will not happen without school staff being more closely involved in the process of forming judgements.

The inspection model throws back to the school the responsibility for the key aspect of improvement identified by Hopkins, Ainscow and West (1994) of 'creating internal conditions to sustain and manage change'. One remarkable feature of our conversations with teachers has been evidence of that resilience that has led them to begin to create these conditions, often despite the setback of a year preoccupied with preparing for inspection as a 'snapshot' summative judgement.

A positive part of the experience that many commented on was the value of conversations with the visiting inspectors, and this led to a clearly expressed wish for a different model of improvement, with more potential for partnership with outside 'experts'. There is only a limited indication in the new *Framework* (OFSTED 1995b) that a model that takes more account of the importance of involvement at school level is being considered.

There is enough evidence to question whether OFSTED's inspection model is the most cost-effective way to improve underachieving schools, and as Hargreaves (1993) warns 'Inspection systems should not be introduced unless it can be shown that they are more effective than alternative approaches to improving the quality of schools.'

CHAPTER ELEVEN

Secondary Schools' Responses to OFSTED: Improvement through Inspection?

by Janet Ouston, Brian Fidler and Peter Earley

The title of this chapter reflects the logo of the new Office for Standards in Education (OFSTED): *Improvement through Inspection*. The research reported here focuses on this issue. Do schools that have been inspected consider the experience to have been helpful to their own development?

Introduction

The successful implementation of the reforms introduced in legislation since 1988 has depended on the capacity of each school to manage its own affairs. The leadership and management provided by head teachers and governing bodies has been of central importance. Schools were expected to draw up School Development Plans (SDPs) to make their priorities explicit and to enable them to review progress.

One of the intentions of the legislation was to make schools more accountable to parents by using market mechanisms to put financial pressures on schools. Whilst a greater accountability to the clients of the school was introduced, direct accountability to others outside the school for professional standards was weakened because of the declining power of Local Educational Authorities. The new pattern of OFSTED inspection was introduced to strengthen professional accountability.

School inspection

The Education Act, 1992, reduced the size and role of HMI and brought into existence the Office for Standards in Education. The new OFSTED inspection process (OFSTED 1994a) was seen as having two components: it served an 'accountability' (or evaluative) purpose through the published inspection report, but it was also intended to act as a spur to, and support for, school development.

The inspection of the first cohort of secondary schools (for pupils aged 11 to 16 or 18) started in Autumn 1993. This chapter is based on the experience of these schools. Inspection of primary schools (for pupils from 5 to 11) started in September 1994.

School Development Planning

In 1986 central government changed the basis of planning and funding professional development for serving teachers. Schools and LEAs were required to draw up plans for professional development based on the assessed needs of schools and teachers and within a pre-determined budget. The concept of institutional needs had been discussed for many years, but most schools found it difficult to identify them. School Development Planning started primarily as a way of identifying training needs for the whole school, although some LEAs saw such plans as having a wider role to play as part of good management practice.

To stimulate such planning, the central government education department, then called the Department of Education and Science (DES) funded a small research project to formulate advice to schools on development planning. Two publications appeared in 1989 and 1991 (DES 1989a, 1991a). Further advice appeared in a book by the two principal researchers (Hargreaves and Hopkins 1991). This built upon work in the 1980s on school self-evaluation as a mechanism for school improvement (McMahon et al. 1984). Such advice, available to all schools, was supplemented in many cases by further material from individual local authorities.

Approaches to planning

School Development Planning has developed in different ways in different schools. This makes it difficult to generalise about practice in general. Undoubtedly there is a spectrum that ranges from plans which might be considered as strategic plans for the whole school (Fidler, Bowles and Hart 1991) to those which are operational plans for implementing the flow of legislation from central government, in particular the National Curriculum.

Plans are produced annually and, according to government guidance, in detail only for one year with 'longer term priorities for the following two or three years .... in *outline*' (DES 1989a). They are likely to fit into a cycle which includes staff development priorities for each financial year beginning in April. As the school year starts in September most plans cover two years in detail and a longer period in outline.

Recent research findings in primary schools have confirmed anecdotal evidence that the practice of development planning is very varied (MacGilchrist and Savage 1994). The extent of the involvement of staff and the extent to which such plans are working documents for action in the school are just two dimensions on which they differ.

The School Development Plan and Inspection

It could be expected that every school would have been involved in school development planning (of varying degrees of sophistication) for a number of years before it was inspected. Indeed given the length of notice which schools have of the inspection, it might have been expected that the most recent School Development Plan would have been produced in the knowledge of a forthcoming inspection, and that it had been influenced by that knowledge. If a school shared OFSTED's priorities for its work and had evaluated its own performance in similar terms to those of the OFSTED inspectors, its priorities for development should be similar to the points for action in the OFSTED report.

Difficulties will arise if there is a serious mismatch between the school's own Development Plan and the points for action identified by the OFSTED inspection team. This will happen if either the school's priorities for action differ from OFSTED's assumptions about the features of an effective school, or that the school is not effective at identifying its own weaknesses through self-evaluation.

The research

The three main research questions were:

- Did schools find the new pattern of OFSTED inspections helpful in their own development?
- What was the relationship between the OFSTED 'action planning process' and the School's Development Plan?
- How could the inspection process aid schools in a more effective and efficient way?

Data were collected on how schools prepared for inspection, their assessment of the value of the verbal debriefing they received at the end of the inspection and the value of the final written report which is delivered six weeks after the inspection. Some details of action planning after the inspection report and opinions about changes to the process were also sought.

It should be appreciated that this study was undertaken at least three months after the inspection when each school had produced its action plan. This may affect perceptions of the process compared to an immediate reaction.

Sample

The schools included in this research were all inspected during the first term, from September to December 1993. Postal questionnaires were sent to the head teachers of all 282 schools in May 1994 and 170 replies were received: a response rate of 60 per cent. (See Appendix A to this chapter for a copy of the questionnaire.)

Findings

The schools responding to the questionnaire came from across the range of English schools as shown in Appendix B to this chapter.

The inspection

The inspection team One of the intentions of the new inspection process was to separate inspection and advice, and to ensure that schools were inspected by inspectors who had no previous contact with the school and hence no preconceptions about it, nor had a continuing advisory role with the school.

Whilst this intention was not expected to be fulfilled in all cases, it was a general expectation of the new inspections. However, just over 40 per cent of team leaders were known to the school before the inspection and in 63 per cent of inspections at least one team member was known to the school.

Pre-inspection preparation The inspection framework was produced and modified shortly before the first inspections. Thus there was some apprehension about the new arrangements. Fear of the consequences of an adverse report led some schools to adopt an adversarial approach to the inspection and the inspectors. This may explain the fact that 87 per cent of schools reported that at least one member of staff attended a pre-inspection preparation course and just under a quarter employed a pre-inspection consultant.

Contribution of the inspection to school development

Contribution of phases of the inspection The relatively long time from notification of inspection until the actual event led the researchers to expect that schools would take steps to overhaul aspects of their work due to be inspected, and that they might make improvements in advance of the actual inspection.

At the end of the inspection the head and senior staff of the school are given a verbal account of the inspection findings. This also provides an opportunity for the staff to ask questions of the inspector and talk informally. Finally, within six weeks of the inspection a written report of 20 to 30 pages is sent to the school which gives quantitative and qualitative findings. This includes reports on the teaching of individual subjects.

The schools were asked to rate the value of each of the three phases: pre-inspection preparation, the inspection itself, and the inspection report. They were asked to assess the contribution that they made to their development on a six-point scale from 0 – *no contribution* to 5 – *major contribution*. Table 11.1 below summarises the replies to these questions:

Table 11.1 Contribution to development of each phase of inspection (the table shows the percentage of schools giving each reply)

Contribution	Pre-inspection Preparation Phase	Verbal Report Phase	Final Contribution Phase
	%	%	%
0 – none	4.7	1.8	2.4
1	12.4	11.2	7.1
2	15.3	18.8	13.5
3	32.4	34.1	37.1
4	27.6	28.2	28.8
5 – major	7.6	5.8	11.2
Total %	100	100	100
Mean	2.89	2.94	3.16
(No. of schools	*170*	*170*	*170)*

Table 11.1 shows that schools in general reported that the Final Report made slightly more contribution to school development than did the verbal report or the preparation for the inspection.

Schools that found one phase helpful in contributing to school development were also likely to report that the other phases were also useful.

Similarly schools that found one phase not useful were likely to report that the others were not useful. These results will be used later in this chapter to create a score indicating the overall contribution of the inspection process to development.

Action planning phase

Timing From receipt of the report schools are allowed 40 working days to produce an Action Plan. Depending on the seriousness and number of the issues which the Action Plan is required to address, this length of time might have been considered inadequate. Only 16 per cent of schools reported that the time allowed for action planning was too short.

Governors' contribution The governing body of the school approve policies and set the general direction for the school. The Action Plan is officially theirs and so heads were asked what part had the governing body played in drawing up the Action Plan. Only 6 per cent of schools reported that their governing bodies had made a major contribution to the Action Plan. The majority of schools reported that their governors had made some contribution, but only one third were above the mid-point of the scale. Nine per cent were said to have made no contribution at all.

Action Plan and School Development Plan As explained above, most schools have a Development Plan which is updated each year. Schools were asked to indicate the extent to which the points made by the inspectors and addressed in the Action Plan overlapped with the existing School Development Plan. In most schools there was some overlap, but only 6 per cent reported a complete overlap, with the inspectors' action points already completely included in the Development Plan. The extent of this overlap and its relationship with other aspects of the survey are discussed later in this chapter.

External advisors and LEA Only 15 per cent of schools used an external adviser to help formulate the Action Plan and half the schools received some help from their LEA.

Implementation of the Plan

Just over 20 per cent of schools employed an external consultant to help implement the Plan and 86 per cent of schools said that their teachers would need additional training to implement some aspects of the Action Plan.

Changes to the OFSTED process

Just under a third of schools thought that additional areas should be included in the inspection process. The following areas were mentioned by schools:

- links with parents, employers and the community
- understanding of the school context and the use of 'value added' statistics
- non National Curriculum subjects
- business studies, economics, vocational courses
- community education
- the sixth form
- the school library
- the extra-curricular programme
- strategic aspects of school management
- the quality of relationships
- provision for children with SEN.

There was disagreement about whether the inspection should be tailored to the individual school. There was also disagreement about how the inspection programme might be revised if resources for inspection were halved. Just under half the schools proposed reducing data collection. These disagreements perhaps reflect the differences between schools in whether they see the inspection process as being mainly for accountability, or mainly for development. Those seeing the process as being for account-ability seem likely to argue for a common approach, whereas those emphasising development will value tailoring the process to the school.

Value of inspection to school development

As already explained, schools were asked to assess how useful the process was to their school's development. In order to create an index of the overall value of the inspection, the answers to the three questions about the phases of the inspection were added together to give a score which ranged from 0 to 15. Schools which found the inspection of little or no value would score low, those which found it very valuable would score high. Table 11.2 shows the distribution of schools on this combined measure. The value of the inspection process was assessed using this score as a measure of the school's response.

Table 11.2 Value of inspection to school development

	N	%
Not valuable (0 – 3)	11	(6.5)
Moderately valuable (4 – 11)	126	(74.1)
Very valuable (12 – 15)	33	(19.4)
Total	170	(100.0)
Mean score	8.99	

Acting head teachers There was a trend for acting heads to be more positive than permanent heads. Nine of the 11 acting heads gave a score of at least 9. The mean score for these heads was 9.9, and for heads in a permanent post 8.9.

Years as a head Newly appointed heads in their first year, and heads who had been in post more than ten years were the most positive. The mean scores are shown in Table 11.3.

Table 11.3 Mean score for value of inspection by years in post

Years in post	Mean score	N
Less than 1	10.4	18
2 to 5	8.2	27
5 to 10	8.8	88
More than 10	9.3	36
Missing		1
Total		*170*

As might be expected, the acting head teachers had all been in post for a short period. The findings set out in Table 11.3 are not accounted for by the positive responses of the acting heads. When the 11 acting heads are excluded from the analysis a similar pattern is found for those in permanent posts.

Team leader Schools where the OFSTED team leader was not known were more positive than those where he or she was known to the school before the inspection. Table 11.4 shows this relationship.

Table 11.4 Team leader known to school

	Mean score	N
Yes	8.5	69
No	9.3	99
Missing		2
Total		*170*

Acting head teachers were less likely to know the team leader than were those in permanent posts, but this does not account for the difference which exists for heads in permanent posts across all years of experience.

Role of the governing body Schools where the governors were reported as contributing to the Action Plan were more likely to be positive about the value of the inspection process as shown in Table 11.5.

Table 11.5   Value of inspection and governors' contribution

Contribution of governors	Mean score	N
Minor (0,1)	8.6	76
Moderate (2,3)	8.9	69
Major (4,5)	10.4	24
Missing		1
Total		170

Compatibility with the School Development Plan Schools were asked how compatible the Action Plan which resulted from the inspection was with the school's existing Development Plan. Those who found the inspection most useful to their school's development were those where there was a moderate overlap. This is shown in Table 11.6.

Table 11.6   Compatibility with the School Development Plan

Relationship with SDPs	Mean score	N
Included (0,1)	8.0	51
Some overlap (2,3)	9.5	90
No overlap (4,5)	9.1	28
Missing		1
Total		170

This is not a surprising finding and might be interpreted along the following lines. Schools that were positive about the inspection found that it confirmed their own perceptions of the school but they gained a new perspective. Schools where there was major overlap between the SDP and the inspection findings felt that 'they had learned nothing new'. Schools where there was no overlap probably found the inspectors failed to share their values and priorities.

Use of external advisor Schools that used an external advisor to help formulate the Action Plan were more positive about the inspection's contribution to school development than were those that did not. This is shown in Table 11.7.

Table 11.7   Use of an external advisor

	Mean score	N
Yes	10.0	26
No	8.8	143
Missing		1
Total		170

Contribution of LEA inspector or advisor to the Action Plan Similarly, schools that were more positive about the contribution of inspection were more likely to have obtained help from the LEA. Table 11.8 shows these results.

Table 11.8   Contribution of the LEA

Contribution of LEA	Mean score	N
None	8.5	86
Minor	9.3	69
Major	9.9	15
Total		*170*

   Interestingly, the use of a consultant to help the school *implement* the Plan was unrelated to their perceptions of the value of the inspection to school development.

Conclusions

This study has shown that most head teachers were positive about the contribution that the OFSTED inspection process had made to their school's development. Only around 6 per cent of heads were quite negative about the contribution.

   Possible tensions between the inspection Action Plan, and the school's own Development Plan, are also suggested. Schools where there was some overlap between the two were much more positive than those where the action points were already included in the school's Plan. These schools possibly felt that they had learned nothing new from what many schools have said was a very stressful experience. This raises issues concerning the ways in which the Inspection Report might be drafted to assist schools in taking their development plans forward, rather than merely confirming their priorities. Schools where there was no overlap were also less positive.

   The findings show that in schools where the inspection process made a major contribution to development, the governing body of the school was involved in formulating the Action Plan, as were external advisors. Other case study evidence points to the fact that those schools which considered that inspections could be of value to them were more likely to report positively on the inspection afterwards. Schools that could envisage ways of making use of the inspection process were more likely to report positively on its value.

   Throughout the interpretation of this study it must be borne in mind that these findings come from the responses of senior members of school staffs – usually the head teacher. Research work currently being undertaken at Oxford Brookes University (reported in Chapter 12) suggests that classroom teachers, at least initially, may be less positive and even rather demoralised by the process. From informal discussion with schools, many report a period of 'post-inspection blues' at the end of the inspection, but this may become lessened as the findings become integrated with the school's work. The study reported here collected data at least three months after the inspection.

Follow up

The researchers are currently following up this group of schools to investigate their perceptions of the influence of inspection two years later. Heads have been asked to reflect on the current impact of the inspection and to report their progress of the inspector's 'issues for action'. This research will be reported in a later publication.

APPENDIX A

BEMAS Improving School Management Initiative

OFSTED Initial Questionnaire (R2)

Please answer the following questions on the basis of the inspection which has taken place under the new OFSTED Framework since August 1993.

Date of inspection..

Information on the School
1. Please give the following information on your school by writing in or circling the appropriate answer.

a) Number of pupils: Main school   ....
                                    Sixth form   ....
                                    Total   ....

b) Status: LEA
                                    Voluntary Controlled
                                    Voluntary Aided
                                    Grant Maintained
                                    CTC
                                    Other

c) Pupils: Percentage (approx) eligible for:
                                    Section 11 support   ....
                                    Free school meals   ....

d) Location: County town/rural
                                    Suburban
                                    Urban
                                    Inner city

e) Designated community school: Yes/No

and the Headteacher
2. Information about the headteacher
       a) permanent post/acting head
       b) male/female
       c) number of years as head of this school ....

122

The Inspection

3. Has any of the inspection team had a previous connection with the school?
   - a) The team leader   Yes/No
   - b) Some/all team members   Yes/No

4. Did you or any of your staff attend any inspection preparation/pre-inspection course(s)?

   Yes/No

5. Did the school employ an external consultant or inspector/advisor to carry out a pre-inspection review of the school?

   Yes/No

6. Did the process of **preparing** for the inspection make a major contribution to your school's development?

   0 1 2 3 4 5

   no contribution   major contribution

7. Did the **verbal feedbacks** received during or shortly after the inspection make a major contribution to your school's development?

   0 1 2 3 4 5

   no contribution   major contribution

8. Did the inspector's **final written report** make a major contribution to your school's development?

   0 1 2 3 4 5

   no contribution   major contribution

9. After receipt of the report, schools have 40 working days to produce their action plan. For your governors was this time:

   Please tick

   Too short ☐
   About right ☐
   Too long ☐

10. To what extent did the governors contribute to the action plan?

    0 1 2 3 4 5

    no contribution   major contribution

11. To what extent was the action plan restating developments already in your school's current development plan (SDP or IDP)?

0 1 2 3 4 5

Action plan already fully included in the current SDP

Action plan focuses on different areas from the current SDP

12. Did the school make use of a consultant or other external advisor to help formulate the action plan?

Yes/No

13. To what extent did an LEA inspector or advisor contribute to the action plan?

Please tick

no contribution	☐
minor contribution	☐
major contribution	☐

14. Does the school expect to employ a consultant or other external advisor to help implement the action plan?

Yes/No

15. Will the implementation of the action plan require any additional staff training or INSET?

Yes/No

16. Are there areas not covered by the OFSTED Framework which you consider should be included?

Yes/No

If Yes, please give brief details.

17. To what extent do you think that the OFSTED Inspection process should be tailored to the individual school?

0 1 2 3 4 5

The same framework should be applied in the same way to all schools

The school should have the opportunity to propose areas of its activity on which it would like a specific comment

18. If the resources devoted to the inspection process had to be reduced by half, how could they be used to best effect to ensure accountability and school development?

Please tick

Keep the present Framework and reduce data collection ☐
Omit some areas from the Framework ☐
Other ☐
Please comment further if you wish.

Name and status of respondent ....

Phone number ....

Would you be willing to answer further questions in a short interview by telephone?

Yes/No

Please indicate if your school would be willing to act as an anonymous case study.

Yes/No/Possibly

Thank you very much for your help.
Please use the space below to provide any other information or comments you wish to make about the OFSTED inspection process.

Please return the completed questionnaire to:
Peter Earley, BEMAS Project NFER,
The Mere, Upton Park,
Slough SL1 2DQ

APPENDIX B

Background data about the schools

Status: LEA (73%), VA and VC (11%), GMS (16%)

Size: Less than 500 (18%), 500–999 (63%), 1,000+ (19%)

Sixth Form: No (48%), Yes (52%)

% pupils eligible for Section 11 support: 0 (67%), 1–10 (19%), 10–50 (10%), 51+ (4%)

% pupils eligible for free meals: 0–5 (20%), 6–10 (22%), 11–25 (26%), 26–50 (24%), 51+ (8%)

School location: Rural (38%), suburban (26%), urban (21%), inner city (15%)

CHAPTER TWELVE

Teachers' Perceptions of Inspections

by Nicola Brimblecombe, Michael Ormston and Marian Shaw

Introduction

The OFSTED inspection process was put in place in order to evaluate the standards and quality of the education on offer in our schools, with the intention of eventual improvement of this offer. It was thus conceived as both an accountability measure and a spur for improvement. In order to inform their judgements about standards and quality, inspectors collect evidence about schools from a variety of sources, but the bulk of their evidence is drawn from observing lessons. Classrooms are complex places, with many different interactions going on simultaneously, and although inspectors are trained in observation (or, more accurately, are tested on their ability to observe), the reliability of the inspection process depends heavily upon the skills of individual inspectors in observing and interpreting what is going on. Classroom teachers are clearly key players, but they have nevertheless been largely ignored by researchers, who have tended to focus on school management teams or on the inspectors themselves.

A pilot study (Ormston and Shaw 1993) indicated that in the run-up to inspection, and during the inspection itself, ordinary classroom teachers felt sidelined. Therefore research was mounted to examine how the OFSTED inspection process was perceived by the teachers themselves. This chapter reports and comments on some of the results of this project so far, and highlights a number of issues that have a potential impact on the outcomes of inspection. Noting that the findings of the pilot study are supported, the chapter explores whether, if teachers lack confidence or feel stressed, they are doing themselves justice while inspectors are in the classroom. If not, we need to ask whether inspectors in those classes are getting an accurate picture of what is going on, or whether the 'inspector' effect is skewing results. This has important implications for the reliability of the report, and ultimately on the picture OFSTED is building up of our schools. Taking a longer view of OFSTED's aim, 'Improvement through Inspection', we have also looked for early indications from teachers as to whether, and how, they intend to change practice.

The chapter first outlines this stage of the research, and then presents some of the results, together with comment. The final section summarises some key issues, and identifies areas which it will be useful to explore in more depth in order to understand whether inspection is achieving its aim.

The research

The first stage of the research project involved 40 secondary and middle schools and 850 teachers; it had two thrusts: a questionnaire survey to 35 schools and an interview-based case study with 5 schools. The sample was drawn from a representative cross-section of LEA and grant maintained schools nationally. All had just completed their inspection, and although some had received their report, most had not. The data was collected in Spring 1994, i.e. the second term of the formal OFSTED process. The sample included almost equal numbers of men and women; their time in teaching and their levels of status were representative of the teaching population.

Through the questionnaire, teachers were asked to recall their feelings on specific occasions before and during inspection, and to identify how they had prepared, or been prepared, for the experience. They were also asked to comment on how the inspectors behaved, and on whether or not they had noticed pupils reacting in any way differently from expected. They were asked to comment, too, on what feedback, if any, they had received. Finally, teachers were asked whether, and in what ways, they intended to change their practice as a result of inspection. The case study interviews provided further explanation and qualification of the apparent trends shown by the questionnaire analysis.

The data was analysed both quantitatively and qualitatively, but, as in any research conducted via self-report, we were aware of the possibility of results being affected by bias or subjectivity. To some extent this was minimised by the triangulation of evidence from different teachers in the same school, and the use of interview as well as questionnaire methods of collecting data.

Results and comment

The interactions in inspection are complex, and in order to achieve clarity, the results here are presented under three main, but interrelated, headings: perceptions, behaviours and intentions to change practice.

Teachers' perceptions of inspection

In an attempt to discover the *real* part that teachers played in the inspection process, we asked our sample to identify what they felt in the run-up to inspection and during it. These results, together with the data about behaviour, have helped build up a picture of the levels of confidence among teachers, and how – or whether – this has affected their performance during inspection. While we found, unsurprisingly, that teachers had mixed feelings about inspection – more feeling wary than unconcerned, but equal numbers of nervous and confident teachers – it was interesting to note that they perceived the period of preparation for inspection with rather more anxiety overall than the time when an inspector was actually in their classes. It would appear, then, that for many teachers the thought of inspection was worse than the actual event. The exceptions were where teachers had an inspector who gave out hostile signals (see next section); even an apparently unfriendly face in the corner of the class had a disproportionately unsettling effect, causing a spiralling of increasing nervousness and decreasing confidence, a point also noted by the NFER study (Dean 1994).

There was an unexpected aspect to this data; while the research did not set out to examine gender associations, significant differences in the way that male and female teachers perceived inspection started to emerge. The figures were examined more closely, and showed a clear tendency for men to have more confidence than women. Almost three times more women than men, for example, reported that they were nervous (before inspection) or worried (during inspection), while 50 per cent more men than women described themselves as confident (both before and during inspection). Although the phenomenon was quite marked, we need to treat the figures with caution, and remember that this survey was based on self-report. Are women *really* more worried about being judged than men? Are they less confident in their own abilities? Or are they, perhaps, more honest, or more articulate in expressing their feelings than their male colleagues? Whichever is the case, school leaders need to recognise that statistically this difference does exist *in the way the staff perceive themselves*, and ensure that *all* members of staff receive the support necessary to build their confidence.

Staff confidence during inspection was also affected by seniority. Those staff in the highest positions (the senior management teams) expressed less worry than their middle managers, who were, in turn, less worried than ordinary classroom teachers. At first this seemed anomalous; why should those with the responsibility of the whole school be less worried about being inspected than their staff? The interviews threw more light on the issue: senior staff tended to be heavily involved with the inspection process from the start, and were able to exercise more control over events, giving them, to some degree, a stronger sense of ownership than was felt elsewhere. It has long been recognised that *not* having control can increase stress (for example, Kyriacou 1990; Punch and Tuettemann 1990) and our research showed that it was not uncommon for staff at lower levels in the school to feel as though inspection was something that was being done to them – a contributory factor in making them feel more stressed; we explore this in more depth elsewhere (Brimblecombe, Ormston and Shaw 1995). The seniority factor, then, is significant, but it is also complicated by the correlation between gender and seniority in secondary schools (see closing section 'Summary and questions for the future').

Most heads would, presumably, wish to ensure that their teachers were performing to the best of their ability when the school was inspected, but it may come as a shock to many heads to realise how powerfully influential they themselves are in enabling staff to feel mentally prepared and confident. Scrutiny of teachers' comments showed that, in preparing staff for inspection, heads were perceived as adopting either reassuring behaviours or scare tactics. Interestingly, the same actions in different schools could have opposite effects; what was perceived as confidence-building in one school increased stress in another. It became clear that the *how* was as important as the *what* (see Shaw, Brimblecombe and Ormston 1995).

In an attempt to find out how accurate a picture the inspectors were seeing, teachers were asked whether they thought that the inspector had seen a lesson that was representative of their normal standard. A disturbing third of our sample said no to this question, and women outnumbered men. Of course, the lesson could have been perceived as either a lower or a higher standard, but the significance of the response lies in the belief that it was different from normal, and therefore gave inspectors a potentially skewed view.

Behaviours

In trying to establish the relationship between what teachers felt and how this affected their performance, our project examined, again through the eyes of the teachers in the sample, what teachers, pupils and inspectors actually did during the inspection process, and our findings throw more light on the complex interactions in the classroom.

Teachers were asked whether, in preparing lessons that they knew (or suspected) an inspector would be watching, they had done anything that was different from normal. Whereas, understandably, most had put in more preparation time than usual, less predictably, a quarter of the teachers planned to deliver a more formal lesson than they would have done. Some did this in the belief that the inspector would consider more didactic lessons to be the 'right' sort – and this was before the much publicised DFE/OFSTED drive for more whole-class teaching. Others changed their approach, becoming 'much more structured and inflexible' in order to 'maintain more control', 'reduce risk' and 'leave less to chance'. The teachers who said they felt unconfident about being inspected were the ones more likely to change their lesson style in this way, but this led sometimes to a spiralling loss of confidence with the increased scrutiny: inspectors tend to focus more closely on what these teachers are doing because there is less to observe in the rest of the classroom.

When we examined whether, and how, teachers changed while the inspectors were in their classes, we found that, overall, one in five of the sample felt that the inspector's presence had caused a change in their own behaviour. Interestingly, though, half the sample believed that their pupils' behaviour changed in the inspector's presence, some pupils being more subdued than normal, and others deliberately playing up. Was this discrepancy real, or did teachers find it easier to recognise behaviour in others than themselves? If it was real, which was cause, and which effect? It might be expected that pupils respond more to their teachers than to an outsider, though this must depend on whether it is a class where other adults are often present. A glimmer of insight was provided by some of the interviewees who said that while they themselves did not *think* they had changed their behaviour, they felt from the responses of their pupils that they probably had.

While head teacher behaviour was seen to play a powerful part in the run-up to inspection, the behaviours of the inspectors were felt by teachers to be highly significant during the actual week of inspection. Observers have long been recognised to affect the observed (for example, Samph 1976, Wragg 1987), and Metcalfe (1994) reports that adjustments in teaching are made as a direct result of having an inspector in class. Nevertheless, OFSTED inspectors are aware of this, and are expected to operate within a code of conduct (OFSTED 1994a) to appear as non-threatening as possible under the circumstances. It was encouraging, therefore, to note that the overwhelmingly large proportion of inspectors were perceived by teachers in our sample as being considerate and helpful; this in itself allowed teachers to gain confidence as the inspection progressed: the fear of the 'unknown' had been dispelled, and teachers in the main reassured. Nevertheless, 8 per cent of the teachers described inspectors' behaviour as being condescending, while 5 per cent said the inspector interfered with the lesson; furthermore, 3 per cent were reported as being openly critical. In schools where this small minority of rogue inspectors operated, they had a disproportionately negative effect, upsetting the delicate balance of emotions in the staffroom. It is hoped that as the inspection process develops, as inspectors understand their role better, and as Registered Inspectors select their team members with more insight, these numbers will shrink further.

Much controversy exists at present around the issue of the sort of feedback that inspectors give to teachers. In our survey, not only did teachers feel cheated when no feedback was given, as was the case in the majority of the lessons recorded in our survey, but they were frequently searching for advice on how to make their jobs more do-able. In order to ensure that the decisions about improvement are made at school level, OFSTED's instructions to inspectors specifically exclude them from offering advice. Nevertheless, it has been hard for teachers to make the adjustment from the old-style LEA inspectors/advisers, or HMI, all of whom evaluated what was going on but then talked about what they had seen and how improvements might be made. Perhaps, without compromising the integrity of the OFSTED process, it may be possible in the future for inspectors to give more support to teachers.

Teachers' intentions to change practice

The aim of the OFSTED process being to improve education, the teachers in our sample were asked whether, and how, they intended to change their practice as a result of inspection. While over a third of the teachers in our sample identified ways in which they intended to change, such intentions need to be treated with caution. This represented teachers' views immediately after their inspection; once engaged with team responses to the Action Plan, they might alter their views. Furthermore, stating intention to change does not, of course, necessarily lead to actual change, and we cannot, either, assume that all change will lead to actual improvement. It is impossible, too, to pinpoint the source of change, as Gray and Wilcox (1994) tease out. Nevertheless, inspection does appear to motivate teachers to make changes that they might otherwise not have done or to speed up changes they intended to make anyway. So what influenced these teachers in resolving to change?

Our research found that those who received no feedback individually were least likely to say they would change; feedback, then, whatever it was, was more likely to affect practice. Bland feedback, however, was found to be least effective in stimulating change, whilst feedback described as constructive, relevant or prescriptive was associated with greatest intention to change. There was also a status association, with nearly half the senior staff, 40 per cent of the middle managers and only 30 per cent of the classroom teachers stating intent to change.

In searching for an explanation, these points were followed up in interview. It would appear that when teachers learnt something new about what was going on in their classrooms, they were able to identify ways in which they could improve their teaching. If, on the other hand, the observer made no comment at all, or gave feedback which was so bland that it did not tell teachers anything new, or give them a different perspective on their work, teachers had no yardstick by which to measure how they were doing. Classroom teachers were the least likely to receive feedback, whereas inspectors are more likely to give considered and substantial feedback to those in managerial positions, with a view to commenting on, for example, departments, or curriculum areas. It is also true to say that individual teachers are protected from OFSTED criticism. Nevertheless, there could be little harm in one-to-one feedback sessions as an *entitlement* for every lesson observed, particularly as this appears to be an important factor in whether teachers decide to change or not. The cost of the extra time invested must surely have a benefit in the overall aims of OFSTED in improving practice?

The commonest targets for change for ordinary classroom teachers were concerned with various aspects of teaching practice, especially differentiation. Improvements in personal organisational aspects of their jobs also came up frequently, while senior and middle managers, unsurprisingly, identified team organisational issues. How these good intentions are translated into actual practice are questions for the future, and the focus of several research teams. Gray and Wilcox's research (1994) suggests that management resolutions are more likely to be implemented than other types, but their research was done on pre-OFSTED inspections.

Summary and questions for the future

This research project has looked at the views of teachers who are being inspected because they are at the heart of the main function of schools, effective teaching and learning. It demonstrates that, while many feel confident about being inspected, a significant number feel insecure, and that this insecurity can be attributed to several causes: the attitude of the head teacher and other senior staff towards inspection, the gender and seniority of staff, and the behaviour of the inspectors. Lack of confidence, the project suggests, is associated with altered behaviour by teachers, abnormal responses from pupils, and a potential skewing of the picture that inspectors see. The issues are complex, and other questions need answering. To what extent, for example, does this skewed picture affect the accuracy of the report? If our data collected during the early stages of the inspection process are representative, they would indicate that a third of teachers feel that they do *not* demonstrate their normal standard of lesson to inspectors. What does this say about the overall picture that OFSTED is building up of schools, bearing in mind that this picture may well affect future policy? Does, in fact, greater familiarity with, and knowledge about, the inspection process in the whole profession give teachers going through it for the first time any greater confidence than those that we sampled in the first stage of our research?

Seniority and gender appear to be important factors in the inspection process, but we do not have a complete picture of these complex issues, nor how they relate to each other. Women come out of the survey as being generally more nervous, statistically, than men, but as senior staff are shown as having more confidence than other teachers, and as there are proportionally more men in senior positions than women, how can we separate the issues with certainty? Indications so far are that women at all levels in schools do tend to express less confidence than their male colleagues, but this is clearly an area that will be examined more closely in the future.

When we looked at whether individual teachers intended to change their practice as a result of inspection, the data revealed that much depended on the sort of feedback that inspectors gave to individual teachers on a personal level. Any feedback was better than none, but bland comments led to less intent to change than helpful, constructive or even critical comments. The process itself came in for criticism, many teachers feeling let down, and even demoralised, by an 'improvement process' that cannot give advice. The research was, of course, carried out on teachers before they had had an opportunity to follow up the issues for action in the development and implementation of an action plan. Some may have felt more overwhelmed and less positive at this initial stage than later when they were actually involved in doing something about the issues raised. Indeed, Ouston, Fidler and Earley (1995) and Metcalfe (1994) have suggested that the attitude was more positive after teachers had started to work on improvements.

It is too early to know whether inspection will lead to long-lasting improvement of learning, but early indications are that comments are taken more seriously in those schools where head teachers create a positive ethos for the staff, treating inspection as a useful consultancy tool which will give insight and inform better practice. The head teacher may create the environment for the inspection, but the views and perceptions of the ordinary classroom teacher are important, because in the end, the school itself must be the locus of improvement, and the classroom is the workshop where this happens.

Part Five: Parents' and Governors' Perspectives

CHAPTER THIRTEEN

Parents' Responses to School Inspections

by Janet Ouston and Val Klenowski

Introduction

This chapter is based on research that explored parents' experience of, and involvement in, the OFSTED inspection process. The research was conducted for the Research and Information into State Education Trust (RISE). It identifies what parents felt worked well and their suggestions for change. The study was small-scale and the findings are indicators to areas of satisfaction and concern.

OFSTED inspections

The Education (Schools) Act 1992 established the new inspection arrangements. These require independent inspections of schools to be undertaken under contract to the Office for Standards in Education (OFSTED). The content and process of the inspection is set out in the *Framework for the Inspection of Schools*, the *Handbook for the Inspection of Schools* and DFE Circular 7/93.

Information is sought from parents in two ways: a meeting with the Registered Inspector (RgI) who leads the inspection team, held before the inspection is undertaken; and a questionnaire to parents which asks about their satisfaction with the school and with their child's education. The meeting with parents should seek parents' views on:

- pupils' standards of work
- the part parents play in the life of the school
- the information which the school provides for parents, including reports
- the help and guidance available to pupils
- the values which the school promotes
- homework
- pupils' behaviour and attendance.

Inspectors are advised that the inclusion of these topics should not prevent the expression of views on other matters. Information from parents via a questionnaire may also be used to provide background information for the inspection.

After the inspection the Registered Inspector is responsible for presenting the findings to the governing body. A full report, and a summary, is then sent to the school, which is required to distribute copies of the summary to all parents. They may purchase a copy of the full report if they wish. The school then prepares an Action Plan in response to the inspection report, and this too is distributed to parents.

The research

A questionnaire and interview survey was undertaken of parents whose children attended 18 English secondary schools inspected in March and April 1994. These schools were all inspected using the OFSTED *Framework*. They included large and small schools, urban, suburban and rural schools, and LEA and grant maintained schools.

The schools' Action Plans were distributed to parents between June and October 1994. Each of the 18 schools agreed to distribute the questionnaires for this study with the Action Plans. A total of 610 questionnaires were returned. Just under a quarter of the respondents completed the three open-ended questions. One of the questions asked whether the parents would be willing to be interviewed. Twenty parents, four of whom were governors, were interviewed, either face-to-face or by telephone, from 11 schools.

The research focused on parents' perceptions of the OFSTED process. How were parents involved in inspections? What do they consider to be strengths of the OFSTED inspection process? What are their suggestions for how parental involvement, and inspection generally, can be improved? Do they think that their involvement is valued by inspectors and by the schools? Some of the issues discussed in this chapter are specific to parent governors, reflecting their more central role, while others concern parents in general.

Multiple data sources were used: questionnaire, interviews and documents. Qualitative analysis of the interviews, the open-ended questions of the questionnaire, inspection reports and Action Plans from some schools was used to identify dominant themes. These are illustrated by quotations from parents' written and spoken comments.

Findings

Parents were asked about their involvement in the inspection process before, during, and after the inspection week. They were asked to describe how they were involved and their personal views about that involvement. Of the parents who responded to the questionnaire over 90 per cent knew that their school was to be inspected before the inspection started. Most parents interviewed (18) said that they were aware in advance that their child's school was to be inspected. The information received by parents from the schools varied in quality, amount, method of communication and timing. The parent governors who were interviewed indicated that they knew well in advance that the school was to be inspected. They were aware of the amount of work that staff were required to do prior to inspection. A parent governor said:

'There was a lot of concern and apprehension prior to inspection. There was information required from the school committees and committee minutes were made available to inspectors.'

Pre-inspection preparation

Twelve of the parents who were interviewed and some of the parents who returned questionnaires felt that the preparation for the inspection on the part of teachers was too paper-based, too stressful and/or too time-consuming. A parent stated:

'A reduction in the paperwork is required. The amount required is frightening, especially for teachers who are concerned with teaching and learning, exam paper work as well! It is immoral to require them to use their time to provide paperwork for inspection purposes. It is another case of wasted money.'

One view that emerged was that there should be no preparation and that inspectors should go into schools unannounced. It was felt that teachers were being pressured by inspection preparation and that either a school was 'running well or it was not.' For example:

'I think the school should not be informed of the date of inspection so that a true reflection of school is obtained. When the date is known it seems that both teachers and children have increased pressure.'

OFSTED Parents' Response Form

Just over three-quarters (77 per cent) of those parents who completed the questionnaire said that they had received a response form and almost all (93 per cent) completed and returned it. Of the 20 parents interviewed only one parent did not receive one of these forms. The number of OFSTED forms returned was considered disappointing in some schools and the design and content of the forms could be improved according to some parents. They felt inhibited by the fact that they were required to sign the form. They described it as 'vague' and 'uninformative' because they had to tick boxes to indicate their responses. Not all schools provided the opportunity for parents to raise concerns or give their views on the school. On the other hand as one parent noted:

'... parents not only filled in the questionnaire (OFSTED response form) but also wrote letters directly to the inspectors and some of the issues raised in those letters have been picked up.'

Where parents were given the opportunity to raise concerns some decided not to because the forms had to be signed and returned to the inspector via the school. Parents were unsure whether confidentiality and anonymity would be ensured, and feared that their comments might have adverse consequences on their children's education. They suggested that response forms should be returned directly to the inspectors, in confidence, to encourage parents to report concerns more honestly.

Meeting with inspectors

The majority of parents (18) who were interviewed understood the purpose of the meeting to be an opportunity for them to 'put their views forward and for inspectors to look at the issues that were raised by parents'. Parents also acknowledged that it was an opportunity for the inspectors to explain what was involved.

The following issues associated with the process of the parents' meeting with the Registered Inspector were identified from the interview and questionnaire data:

- the need for clear and accurate information about the meeting to be communicated directly to all parents;

- greater encouragement for a larger and more representative sample of parents to attend;
- a more careful consideration of the timing of the meeting to encourage maximum attendance from a cross-section of parents;
- the preservation of confidentiality and anonymity for parents in their communication of information to the inspectors;
- the opportunity for parents to contribute issues for discussion and for these to be included on the meeting agenda; and,
- a meeting procedure which encourages parents to express their views.

In some cases the meeting with the inspectors was described as 'very open'. A parent explained how:

> ' ... parents were able to criticise, add or defend the issues on the agenda. Parents were not shy about raising issues that they were concerned about. On the whole they were not things that were destructive – they were raised in quite a constructive way.'

The overall impression gained from the parents interviewed, however, was that 'parents were guarded and diplomatic.' This was particularly the case where parents themselves were involved in the teaching profession, or where teachers at the school were present at the meeting.

Inspection week

During the inspection week parents were not actively involved unless they were governors. A parent governor described his participation as very structured. He attended a two hour meeting with four inspectors, the head teacher, the chair of governors and five other governors. In his words:

> 'In effect what they did was grill us on various aspects of the school – aims of the school, our understanding of what was going on. The inspectors asked a question and we gave them an answer.'

Issues such as discipline to finance were covered during this meeting and the parent governor felt that the inspectors wanted to know how well the governors understood the school's operations.

During the inspection

Parents were aware that during the inspection a wide range of students were interviewed by inspectors. One explained:

> 'The children were chosen by the school according to criteria drawn up by

inspectors – they had to produce all their homework and notebooks. The students were of varying ability. It wasn't left to the school to choose. It had to be a cross-section. The children were aware that the inspectors were around but not in an intrusive way.'

Reports

The summary and final reports prepared by the Registered Inspector reflect the collective view of the whole inspection team, and are sent to the school. The summary should be distributed to all parents. The full report can be obtained from the school, which is allowed to charge the cost of photocopying.

All parents who were interviewed received a copy of the summary report and just under 90 per cent of the parents who responded to the questionnaire said that they had received it. In most cases parents were also aware that they could purchase or have access to the full report if they wanted. Just under a quarter (23 per cent) of the parents who completed the questionnaire obtained a copy of the full report. Some parents objected to having to pay for it.

Parental views about whether the report reflected the right issues and their perceptions of whether their input was valued varied from school to school. Several parents commented on the 'bland nature of the summary report': the report appeared to gloss over issues. For example, one parent indicated that the report was full of statistics yet offered very few explanations.

In some schools parents believed that there were contradictions between the summary and full reports. They wanted more information about the meanings of some parts of the report, such as clarification of these types of statements: 'satisfactory but below the national average'. Other dissatisfactions related to issues raised by parents which they felt were not fully covered in the report. For example, at one school a parent was critical of the presentation of the summary report where the school had prefaced it with positive quotations from the full report. She was disappointed that the inspectors did not portray accurately issues of concern to parents. She concluded that the inspection was disappointing, given the summary report and the information which was published in the local newspapers. She said that some teachers had lost control of their classes and needed help and support. She was also concerned about bullying. Yet the outcome of inspection was a denial of these problems; an opportunity to be honest about them was lost.

When asked whether the report reflected the right issues eleven interviewees thought that this was the case. Similarly, 91 per cent of those returning the questionnaires indicated that inspections looked at the right aspects. The issues identified as being important included: student behaviour, discipline, bullying; the quality of work and educational standards; exam results; teaching standards; areas of specific subject curriculum weakness; religious education; homework; Special Education Needs; assessment and reporting; school ethos; student/teacher relations; class sizes; school management; attendance and truanting; facilities; extra-curricular activities; safety issues; drugs; poor performance of boys and primary/secondary transfer.

There were supportive comments for the inspectors' reports:

> 'The right issues were addressed fully in the report. The report was fair, accurate and highlighted recognisable issues.'

Some parent governors were able to identify issues of concern from the report that they felt were important. For these parent governors the reports will be a useful source of evidence to assist them in being more effective:

> 'The report reflects the right issues, the report highlighted a number of things ... as a parent governor I had feelings about and a lot of governors would agree. One thing is stricter reading standards. That's substantiated with evidence ... reading results and comments in the report were a shock. We had realised that reading was a problem but we had not realised the extent of the problem. On the whole the report reflects the right issues. It confirms the strengths and highlights the areas for improvement. I think that the other weaknesses will now be put right. They will have to be put right. The greatest difficulty is English as a second language and to a certain extent ethnicity.'

For other parents the report did not reflect the right issues. One parent explained that what he considered to be the 'simple issues' were reported. To illustrate what he meant he referred to the issue of homework and the need for students to use their homework diaries. He considered this issue to be less important than the issue of checking to see what the student had learnt from completing the homework or if indeed the student had completed the homework.

The following themes emerged from the questionnaire responses concerning aspects of the school's work which were important to parents, but not inspected. They wanted more comment and discussion on particular issues such as: homework; equal opportunities; Special Educational Needs; standards of education; bullying; teachers who were not performing well; sports participation and examination results.

Several parents were critical of the biased nature of what the inspectors saw and the consequent, 'coloured' report. One of these parents suggested that 'Inspectors should concentrate on parents' attitude to school and should spend time on quizzing them.' They felt that the teachers and students were on their best behaviour during the inspection and that inspectors did not get a true impression of the school. The image portrayed by some parents at the meeting was also considered by others to be 'too perfect' or 'too positive'. This had led to what some parents perceived as a biased report.

Almost a quarter (23 per cent) of the parents who responded to the questionnaire said that they were surprised by something in the report. Some of these issues were: standards in relation to the national norm; the emphasis on RE; some low or unsatisfactory teaching standards and low achievement of boys.

Action planning

After the inspection, the school and its governing body have to develop an Action Plan based on the inspectors' findings. There was limited parental involvement in the development of the Action Plan. The parent governors' involvement consisted of attendance at meetings after the inspection to discuss the strengths and the weaknesses of the school. In most schools, staff were responsible for the production of the Action Plan which was then presented to the governing body for approval.

Generally parents were aware of the Action Plan and believed that they would be able to monitor the Plan when it was discussed at the annual parents' meeting. Many parents and parent governors perceived the action planning phase to be a strength because it forced the school, the governors, the individual staff to revisit certain issues and provided an opportunity for whole-school evaluation. A parent governor noted how the action planning had 'pulled the staff together' for the common purposes of developing whole-school policy on issues like reading standards. In some situations this phase caused schools to confront problems that they had actually discovered for themselves which had now been substantiated by the inspection process. Many parents felt that if the Action Plan did not take up the issues then it would be a missed opportunity.

The time schedule of the inspection process created problems for some governing bodies. Parent governors wanted more time to consider the Action Plan before they were required to present it. For example, in nine of the schools there was pressure to finalise arrangements for the distribution of the Action Plan in the last week of term. For four schools, the 40 days they are allowed to prepare the Action Plan was broken by the summer holidays and momentum was lost. These schools had to postpone the governors' meeting on the Action Plan until the beginning of September, which meant that it was not distributed until the second or third week of September.

Conclusions

There were certain strengths and suggestions for improvement of the inspection process identified by parents. Parents' concerns related to issues of cost-effectiveness, impact of inspections on the school and level of their involvement.

Perceived strengths

Parents were positive about many aspects of the OFSTED inspection process.

- Parents valued the requirement for inspectors to base their judgements on evidence.
- For schools with an unjustified 'bad' reputation parents particularly judged the inspection to be worthwhile because a favourable report offered support to those parents who might have had doubts about the school.
- The opportunity to voice concerns to an external body was also seen as positive.
- The role for parents and governors in the monitoring of the implementation of the Action Plan was seen as an added strength. This governor explained: 'Issues such as homework that have been identified will now need to be acted upon. Previously the governors didn't have the professional support to ensure that such action was taken.'
- The inspection process was seen as a catalyst for change and was valued where it was needed. For example: 'The school was aware of the need for change but the inspection process has caused the school to do more about it. A lot of staff have been lost and this will be an opportunity for the head to strengthen weak areas and really develop areas that have become stale. It's easy for teachers to get into a rut and lose their effectiveness.'
- Action had to be taken and this pleased parents. In some schools the pastoral care policy had been described as unsatisfactory: the requirement for these schools was to develop clear policies on bullying, homework and discipline. This was considered to be 'a step in the right direction'.
- In schools where the Registered Inspectors made themselves available and were open to parents' views it was considered a strength of the process: 'The inspector made it clear that he was willing to accept information from parents either in written form or would speak to them directly.'
- The interviews with students were also seen as positive: 'I was

astonished at how much interest the inspectors took in the young people they interviewed. I can't recall a time in my teaching career where inspectors talked to children. So it was interesting that they were looking at a student viewpoint as well as a teacher and parent viewpoint of the institution.'

- The opportunity for parents to be involved was welcomed. Where they were kept informed throughout the inspection process, and where the head welcomed the inspection, parental involvement was facilitated. In some schools parents were able to contribute items to the meeting agenda, these included: bullying; exam preparation; teaching of foreign languages; drug problems in the school and community; the merit certificate system; safety, smoking and the need for teacher supervision on buses; sexism and macho image of a particular subject department; uniform; provision for special education needs and lack of facilities.

Suggested improvements

Parents suggested some improvements for the OFSTED response form and the meeting with inspectors.

- They wanted more notice of the date and time of the meeting so that they could make the necessary arrangements to enable them to attend.
- They suggested that the importance of the meeting should be more fully explained to encourage attendance.
- More opportunities to put their views forward without the constraints of a rigidly structured agenda were suggested. It was important, they felt, for the inspectors to understand the special features of their children's schools.
- Many parents commented on the stress experienced by staff and pupils during the inspection process. A reduction in paperwork required by inspectors was proposed. Some parents reported that teachers were exhausted by the end of the inspection. One parent noted that the exhaustion was ' ... as much to do with tension as to do with the time of the year that it came. The stress levels were very much increased for the teaching staff ... the teachers were expected to put on as many as eight performances per day, five days a week and to be at peak form every day. The inspectors actually looked at 150 lessons, 35 registration periods and a huge range of extra-curricular activities!'
- Parent governors in particular wanted greater involvement of the governing body to ensure that 'everybody speaks with one voice'. It was suggested that a governor, a parent or a staff member should be a

member of the inspection team. This member should be a spokesperson for parents and should be chosen independently of the head. He or she could offer information, explanation or clarify points for inspectors, ask questions and raise common parental concerns.

- A parents' meeting to be held by the school before the meeting with the inspector was another suggestion for improvement. This meeting could give parents an opportunity to clarify their ideas before meeting with the inspectors and provide them with an explanation of how the inspection would be undertaken.
- Inspectors should identify more accurately the areas for improvement, according to some parents. Weaknesses were not identified nor were the strengths of some schools clearly acknowledged.
- For the majority of parents an essential addition to the process was the need for a post-inspection meeting with the parents. For example one parent wrote: 'It may have been helpful to have a meeting after the inspection, with the Inspectors. Education is very complicated with various levels being quoted. That is, it would be clearer to have the report verbally as well, and also for parents to ask any questions raised by the report.'
- Parents want to be assured that future inspections will preserve the continuity with this initial inspection. Parents wanted to know; 'How will continuity be preserved? Will the same OFSTED team carry out the inspection of the same school in four years' time?'

Parents' concerns

Parental concerns related to: the cost of inspection, the level of involvement of parents, the relations between the school and parents, perceptions of OFSTED, the impact of inspectors on the school and the role conflict for parent governors in the inspection process.

- The cost-effectiveness of the inspection process was questioned and the overall cost of the inspection was a concern. Some parents felt the money could have been better used by the schools to implement their existing Development Plan.
- Some parents did not want any more involvement in the inspection process and cautioned against further parental participation: 'I think that the parents would get in the way. The head, the teachers and the inspectors are the professionals and they need to get on with it.'
- Others were concerned, about the inspection itself, while some felt that the educationalists were the professionals and should be left to get on with the work of teaching and learning. It was described as 'cosmetic

parental involvement' by some who felt that schools 'only pay lip service to the concept'. It was perceived that schools and educationalists did not want further involvement of parents (particularly their increased access to information) as this could slow down educational decision-making.

- An unfavourable report can have a negative impact on the relations between the school and parents. The inspection had confirmed some parents' beliefs: 'I know the school needs improvement and this proved it.'
- Parents expressed their concern regarding the image and overall effect of the inspection on the school. They spoke of 'the threat of OFSTED' and in some schools 'the inspectors were seen as the enemy'. Parents indicated that if OFSTED were to be a vehicle for change then: '... it needs to be less stressful for teachers. It needs to be supportive of teachers to do the job.' Many parents were concerned that: 'With the new system a lot of teachers have had the stuffing knocked out of them and have been undervalued!'
- Parents were concerned that the inspectors might not see the school as it would normally be. For example: '... the children were better behaved than normal. Were the inspectors aware of their impact?' Some parents noted increased marking by some teachers and, in another school, a parent noted 'an overenthusiastic use of merit certificates' to improve student behaviour before inspection.
- During the inspection process a role conflict emerged for parent governors. They are members of the governing body and therefore have a legal responsibility for the performance of the school, so they too, are being inspected. The parent governors who were interviewed felt obliged to highlight positive aspects of the school while their anxieties as parents were not raised because it might have been considered to be disloyal to the school. To be too frank about the school's weaknesses was seen as conflicting with the role of parent governor. As one parent governor stated: 'The inspectors' role is to find out what the weaknesses are, it is not up to the governors to tell the inspectors. If we do their job for them, then in a way they are going to be side-tracked and they might miss the real issues, which could be catastrophic.'
- This role conflict also emerged for parent governors during the parents' meeting with the inspectors. It felt inappropriate for parent governors to debate parental issues in such a public forum.

Value of parental involvement

Of the parents who were interviewed 12 felt that their views were valued by the inspectors and the school. Nearly all the parents (97 per cent) who attended the parents' meeting reported that the inspectors were interested in their views. The four parent governors who were interviewed felt that they were able to provide valuable information to the inspectors. In one school the parent governors were able to give the background and history of the school to the inspectors to explain the exam results. In this way the parent governors felt that they were educating the inspectors.

This report is based on a small-scale study with a number of constraints. The researchers have been cautious in their interpretation of the data and in the formation of their conclusions. This study could be considered as a pilot study for a larger project that could consider some of the issues that have emerged from this study. Areas for further research include:

- How to involve parents to an extent that is beneficial and appropriate for all?
- What role should the parent governor fulfil in the inspection process?
- How can communication between school and parents be improved?
- Why is parents' attendance at the meeting with the Registered Inspector rather poor?
- Why do so few parents request a copy of the full inspectors' report?
- Do the outcomes from the inspection justify the costs involved?
- To what extent are schools prevented from implementing their Action Plans due to a shortage of resources?

Acknowledgement

The research on which this article is based was undertaken for the Research and Information on State Education Trust (RISE). The researchers wish to acknowledge the financial support provided by the Nuffield Foundation.

Note

The Research and Information on State Education Trust (RISE) is based at 54 Broadwalk, London E18 2DW.

CHAPTER FOURTEEN

The OFSTED Experience: A Governors' Eye View

by Maureen O'Connor

As the OFSTED inspection process has bedded itself down in the secondary schools and been launched, not without hiccups, in the primary sector, I have had contact professionally with a number of governors who had been in the first cohorts of schools to go through the OFSTED mill. As chair of governors of a 13 to 18 upper school I also had personal experience of one of the first OFSTED inspections.

Early in 1994 a group of secondary governors met at a conference sponsored by the Trustees of Research and Information on State Education (RISE) and funded by the Nuffield Foundation. This meeting brought together governors of schools which had experienced an inspection by OFSTED during the Autumn Term, 1993. At the end of 1994 I interviewed a number of governors of primary schools in the group which had been inspected during the Autumn of that year when the new system was introduced to the primary sector.

The role of governors is important in the OFSTED procedure. Governors have a responsibility (DFE Circular 7/93) to:

- Agree a specification for the inspection.
- Inform parents, the LEA or Secretary of State, Foundation if relevant, and in the case of secondary schools, the local Training and Enterprise Council and representatives of the local business community that the inspection will take place.
- Arrange the meeting between the Registered Inspector (RgI) and parents.
- With the staff of the school, offer the RgI every opportunity to make a full and fair assessment of the school by providing the necessary

documents, ready access to lessons and school activities and discussions with individuals and groups of governors, staff and pupils.

- Discuss with the RgI the main findings of the report.
- Make arrangements for the parents of every pupil to be sent a copy of the summary report; make reasonable arrangements for the report and the summary to be available for inspection by the public; provide any person who asks for it with a copy of the report.
- Decide on and carry out an Action Plan arising from the inspection. This must be sent to the parents, employees, OFSTED, the LEA or Secretary of State, the Foundation if relevant and the local TEC. Progress on the implementation of the Action Plan must be reported in the governors' annual report to parents.

One aim of the RISE conference was to bring governors of recently inspected schools together in the hope that they would be able to identify and publicise any variations in the way OFSTED inspections have been conducted, particularly in relation to the role of governors in the inspection and to suggest possible improvements with a view to clarifying good practice. The conference also offered an opportunity for governors to discuss the formulation and implementation of the Action Plan they are required to produce.

Chairs of governors from 100 schools which had been inspected during the Autumn Term of 1993 were invited to the conference in London in April 1994. Twenty-five representatives from 23 schools attended, most from mixed comprehensive schools, one from a grammar school, one from a boys' secondary modern school. Three of the schools represented were grant maintained and two were voluntary aided.

There was a wide geographical spread of delegates. Thirteen of the delegates were chairs of their governing bodies and there was a representative spread of LEA nominees, co-opted and parent governors and one Foundation governor from a voluntary aided school. The conference was also attended by a small group of RISE trustees and others, some of whom were also governors.

Introducing the conference the President of the Campaign for the Advancement of State Education (CASE), Joan Sallis, said it was important that if school governors were to be held responsible for school improvement after an OFSTED inspection they should have had genuine, hands-on involvement beforehand. Governors should have been involved in the process of inspection from the beginning and the process should have been a creative one for school improvement and for the self-criticism which governing bodies should embrace.

Margaret Williamson, HMI, said that OFSTED had been keen to evaluate the new inspection process from day one. The first evaluation,

A *Focus on Quality*, produced in co-operation with consultants Coopers & Lybrand, was based on OFSTED's own evidence drawn from its first 100 secondary inspections in late 1993, and from the reactions of 100 head teachers, 68 individual governors and 83 groups of school staff.

Four key questions were posed:

- How helpful was the newly published *Framework* and *Handbook* to those being inspected?
- How satisfied were governors, heads and staff with the overall management and conduct of the inspections?
- How manageable is the inspection model?
- How should OFSTED revise and refine the model in the light of first reactions to the new system?

Margaret Williamson said that some of the initial difficulties of the new system were caused by the speed at which is was introduced. OFSTED had found that in only one third of schools were governors directly involved in preparation for the inspection and in few were governors involved in the preparation of the specification, this being left in most cases to heads.

The majority of Registered Inspectors had held meetings with representatives of the governing body, either during the inspection or at the time of the parents' meeting. Oral evidence of the work of governors was largely reflected through discussions with the chair of governors, though a small number of Registered Inspectors tried to involve other governors to gather a wider range of views.

Feedback to governors often took the form of a shortened version of the oral report to heads and senior staff. Reactions from governors to these sessions were mixed. A number of chairs of governors wanted clearer guidance from the Registered Inspector of what to expect from the oral feedback. Some had complained that they found it difficult to absorb the range of information and judgements.

Some governors had complained about the amount of educational jargon included in reports. One sought to avoid an 'issues for action' section for fear of unfavourable parental reaction. Others requested help in the formulation of Action Plans. On the publication of the final report, some schools complained about the precise wording and about the brevity of the summary. Registered Inspectors have been asked to improve the consistency and readability of the summary reports which go to parents.

Margaret Williamson concluded that from OFSTED's point of view the new system had got off to a reasonably good start but that there were still issues to be tackled. Schools should not be left feeling stressed or swamped by the inspection procedure, she said. The proof of the success of the new system, she said, would lie in evidence of genuine school improvement resulting from it.

Delegates were asked in their discussion groups to complete a questionnaire giving some indication of how they had been involved in the inspection process at their schools. Thirteen of those present were chairs of governors.

The questionnaire revealed the following information:

- Only two of the 22 governors responding felt they had not been made aware of their responsibilities as governors for the inspection.
- Eight governors felt that they had been excluded from the preparation for the inspection.
- Less than half of the respondents had seen the documentation involved in the preparation work for the inspection: six had specifically seen the financial questionnaire, and four had seen the head teacher's form.
- The majority of governors had met the Registered Inspector before the inspection, half the meetings taking place with governors alone, half with members of the school's senior management team present.
- Half the governors had met the inspectors during the course of the inspection, either individually or in a group, and in three cases, in both ways.
- Just over half the governors had learned what issues had been raised at the parents' meeting. Most of those who did not were chairs of governors but not parent governors
- Without exception the Registered Inspector reported back to the whole governing body
- Governors' views on the inspection process had been sought by OFSTED evaluators in seven schools through discussion and in two cases by questionnaire.
- With only one exception the governors present had been involved in compiling the school's Action Plan following the inspection.
- Arrangements for writing the Action Plan varied widely: in three schools the head teacher drafted the Plan, in one the chair did so, but in most individual governors and the senior management team or a specially constituted working group of governors and staff drew up the Plan. In one school the whole governing body and the senior management team compiled the Plan.
- Action Plans were split equally between those which were based on the points for action in the summary report, and those which were based on the issues raised in the full report.
- Not all governors knew how many parents had asked for a full copy of the report. Two schools had had 20 requests, one had had ten, the rest had had one or two or none at all.

There was a general feeling amongst all the governors I spoke to in 1994 that the inspection had been a largely positive process. Governing bodies had found that it clarified their role and responsibilities and that it generally strengthened relationships between governors, pulling less active members into the team, and between head teachers and their governors. Relationships with staff had often improved. Some had found that the process increased the level of trust between school and parents. Many governors felt that their right to make strategic decisions and to monitor the school had been clarified, as had their right to be involved in curriculum matters. A school which had been threatened with closure felt that their report endorsed their right to 'stay alive'.

Many governors expressed the view that the process had been highly educative for them: it spelled out their legal duties and responsibilities, informed them much more fully about the work of the school, gave them a means to identify weaknesses which had not previously been discussed openly and in many ways acted as a catalyst for future development. As one said: 'It gave us the key to the schoolroom door'. Many governors said that they had been empowered by the inspection which had made their role transparent to head, staff and parents. One governor welcomed the 'free audit'. Others claimed that management and financial procedures had been sharpened by the experience. The *Handbook* was felt to be an extremely useful 'guide to good practice'.

But a primary governor, while accepting that governors are inevitably involved in the inspection process, admitted to a sense of shock. 'I think volunteers are not used to the idea that their work will come under scrutiny'. She agreed with others that the process was a valuable one which clarified the governors' responsibilities and brought them into closer contact with the school than had perhaps been the case before.

A chair of governors who made it her business to be in school every day during the inspection said that she saw her function as making sure that the head and the staff were as happy as they could be. 'It is a stressful time, and I think the governors can provide support as well as taking part in the interviews which the Registered Inspector requires'.

Many schools mentioned the 'hang-over' period after the inspectors had gone. A governor suggested providing a party on the last day to dissipate the tension, but most schools found that post-inspection syndrome lasted longer than that. Although a few governors said that their reports hadn't told them anything new, they appreciated having professional confirmation that the school was heading in the right direction. A 'second opinion' was highly valued.

Reactions were not entirely positive. Many governors complained of the very short time-scale on which their early inspections had been run. One school had been hit by a flu epidemic in the two weeks before the inspectors' arrival and felt ill-prepared as a result. There were also complaints about the volume of paperwork required, and the lack of resources to meet OFSTED's demands both before and after the inspection and the levels of stress imposed on heads and staff.

There was some concern about the composition of inspection teams. A grant maintained school governor felt that it was unacceptable to be inspected by a team from their previous local authority. Others felt that local authority teams should not inspect in their own area (although, conversely, some governors felt that a team which knew the school previously would make a fairer inspection). Two governors were concerned about specific team members whom they had tried to have removed because of their previous relationships with the school. Conflict of interest was held to be a potentially serious problem.

There was criticism of the way in which the inspection teams performed. 'Private' teams were held to be less well integrated than LEA teams. There was dissatisfaction with the performance of the Lay Inspector in several schools. Staff had expressed reservations about the sometimes clumsy way in which lessons were observed and feedback presented. Governors felt that there were weaknesses in communication throughout the process, sometimes between inspection teams and the school, sometimes between heads and chairs of governors. The feeling was strongly expressed that if governors are to be inspected, they must be fully integrated into the process and all communications addressed to them must reach them.

Language was an area of serious difficulty too for many schools as a whole and for governors in particular. 'Inspectors come into school with OFSTED-speak tripping off their tongues, but schools are not yet familiar with the jargon' a primary head told me. 'There is confusion about the 'national expectations'' said another. 'Expectation is not the same as an average. It actually ought to be something to aim at, something you strive for. The language is actually being misused and no one, not even teachers, understands exactly what is meant'. Others complained that governors had been 'bemused' at their meeting to hear the Registered Inspector introduce the report, or that parents had been unable to make sense of the summary they have to be presented with. 'People just don't realise that words like 'sound' and 'satisfactory' are actually intended to be complimentary' one head commented. 'It is very difficult for lay people to come to terms with the language of these reports' said another head. 'Our governors found the whole report bland and could barely distinguish between praise and criticism'. There is nothing to stop schools sending out their own version to parents in plain English, another school concluded, although they thought it wise not to gloss over the criticism. But with some schools complaining already about the cost of reproducing and circulating the summary, that may not always be feasible. There is a strong feeling amongst heads that OFSTED should bear those costs anyway.

Other governors complained that the language used in reports was often 'bland', others that it was 'alienating and meaningless'. There was general agreement that terms such as 'satisfactory', 'good' and 'poor' should be more carefully defined. Does 'satisfactory' mean up to standard?

There were complaints that reports contained glaring omissions and inaccuracies: a school facing severe difficulties on two sites did not have this factor acknowledged; at another, inspectors had informed the head verbally of a fire risk but not included it in their report – shortly afterwards there was a fire. This led governors to believe that the process was too rushed and tended to give only a 'snapshot' view of a school, with little account taken of local issues and conditions.

There were also complaints that there were discrepancies between feedback to staff after a classroom observation, verbal feedback to management teams and governors, and the final published report and summary. There was, overall, too much emphasis on failure and too little on success.

The governors at the RISE conference came up with the following list of points which they felt would improve the process (not in any order of priority):

- Less bureaucracy and paperwork would assist schools, as would help with the expense of an inspection.
- Better communication systems, particularly with governors, would make it easier for them to play their full role in the process. OFSTED should ensure that communications addressed to chairs of governors actually reach them.
- The language in which reports and summaries are written should be clearer and better defined. Reports should emphasise success as well as failure.
- The feedback to governors should be based on a written, not an oral, draft and should never be read to them.
- The inspectors should be willing to take account of schools' comments on the report at the feedback sessions.
- The inspection process should be longer and less rushed, and the opportunity taken for offering professional advice to staff.
- More attention should be paid to dealing adequately with specialist areas like special needs, personal and social education and non-National Curriculum subjects.
- Lay Inspectors should be selected and trained more carefully.
- Governors should be offered training 'pre-OFSTED'.
- Communication with parents should be at a more appropriate level, especially in areas where more than one language is spoken.

The Action Plan was of serious concern to governors as they felt that the responsibility for drawing it up and monitoring its implementation was a heavy one. Most governors felt that drawing up a Plan was a helpful exercise, enabling schools to prioritise future improvements and clarify objectives. Some felt that the 40 days allowed was too short. Several commented on the potential for integrating the Action Plan with the school's existing Development Plan as a way of clarifying development, although some felt that there was some conflict here.

Plans are now being dutifully produced by heads and governors all over the country but there is genuine astonishment that there is no apparent means of ensuring that OFSTED – or anyone else – follow these up. Many schools felt that post-OFSTED help and advice should be provided, but they had little optimism that their local authority would be able to provide what was needed and none that OFSTED would ever be back to check on the outcome of their Action Plan. Most governing bodies had themselves agreed to some form of monitoring of the implementation of the Plan over time.

Some schools had produced two Action Plans, a long version for internal use and a summary for parents, although it is not clear whether this is acceptable to OFSTED.

Some schools found the OFSTED language on Action Plans opaque and in general it was felt that schools needed far more guidance than they had been offered in drawing up a Plan acceptable to OFSTED, resourcing it and monitoring its implementation. This reflected the plea for greater professional guidance on school improvement during the inspection process. Some governors said that they had relied heavily on the school's senior management in drawing up the Plan.

Some issues, such as the common difficulties over collective worship, had been deliberately fudged in Action Plans.

There was a general feeling that the divorce of inspection from advice meant that schools where problems had been identified were left without support in matters of school improvement, and there was some anger that no account was being taken of the financial implications of the inspection process or school improvement.

Governors at the RISE conference made the following suggestions for improvement:

- The Registered Inspector should receive a copy of the Action Plan.
- Means should be found to provide the resources needed to implement an Action Plan after an inspection.
- There is a need for more support and training for governors and staff in the drawing up and implementation of an Action Plan.

Many governors I spoke to felt that their OFSTED inspection had been a very positive experience both for them and for the schools they represented. They had constructive criticisms about the way in which the process, and its follow up Action Plan phase could be improved. They also had some philosophical objection to the divorce between the inspection process and the advisory and support services which they felt schools needed if they were to make constructive use of the inspections process and improve the schools for which they were responsible. They also had reservations about the way in which the new procedures put them, as amateur, unpaid volunteers, into a highly responsible and accountable role, which was highly vulnerable to adverse comment. Although few went as far as one delegate who insisted that the purpose of the system was to 'create fear and panic', most agreed with another who said: 'there should be no inspection without support!'

My informal research on schools which had been inspected resulted in a brief check-list for governors which could be of interest to all those schools which have yet to endure trial by OFSTED.

When the letter arrives

- Read the *Framework for Inspection*.
- Consider whether governors need training and where that is available. Many LEAs are providing governor training.
- Make quite sure the governing body understands its responsibilities and has its own policy and other documents in order.

Before the inspection

- Consider having a single governor, possibly the chair, to handle all aspects of the inspection.
- Work with the head on the specification form.
- Consider the organisation of the parents' meeting with the head, especially who should explain the inspection process and introduce the Registered Inspector.
- Plan for the chair's meeting with the Registered Inspector and consider whether other governors should be involved.
- Consider how you monitor the effect of the governing body's decisions, particularly financial decisions, on the school's effectiveness.

Note

The Research and Information on State Education Trust (RISE) is based at 54 Broadwalk, London E18 2DW.

Part Six: The Political Perspective

CHAPTER FIFTEEN

Conservative, Labour and Liberal Democrat Policies

by Gillian Shephard, David Blunkett and Don Foster

Gillian Shephard

The Government is committed to the inspection of all state schools within a four-year cycle. This is a massive undertaking. It means that by July 1998 around 25,000 schools will have been the subject of full-scale independent inspections. All reports will be made public. All parents will receive a summary of the reports. All governing bodies will have to act on the inspection reports and produce Action Plans to address any weaknesses recorded in the report.

Inspections are the centre-piece of the Government's school improvement programme. We are committed to them. They keep parents and the public informed on progress in our schools. They provide professional feedback to governors and staff on the school's strengths and weaknesses and they enable action to be taken where improvement is needed.

For example there have been around 60 schools formally identified as failing under the new inspection measures, as at early June 1995. These schools need help: they are now getting it. The help comes from the follow-up reports of inspectors, from extra support from the LEA, from advice by the Department and other bodies or individuals and, most importantly, from a desire by the school itself to improve. Sometimes it takes an authoritative outside view to force a school to look searchingly at its performance and to target its energies and resources where they are most needed.

By Easter 1995 one failing school had already been turned round. OFSTED report that others are making good progress. We know that some will eventually have to close or may need to be taken over by an Education Association. This must be preferable to allowing children to continue to receive poor education.

It is unlikely that this action or improvement would have been possible without a full-scale, rigorous and independent inspection system. In the past HMI would only have been able to undertake around 100 inspections a year: at that rate a primary school might wait 200 years for an inspection and a secondary 60 years. Too many generations of children would have suffered whilst schools sank into slow and unpublicised decline. Contrast this with the new system: already by Easter 1995 nearly 3,300 schools had been inspected under the new arrangements.

This Government is not just committed to inspection: we believe that to be effective it must be based on an independent system with its findings made public. Some LEAs did, and still do, have inspection arrangements. But in not enough cases were these seen as really independent. There was no national consistency about their inspection reports. Too many reports were not published or made easily available. Under the new arrangements all schools know exactly how they will be inspected and all reports must be rapidly published. The new *Framework of Inspection* is now in virtually every head teacher's bookcase. It ensures that we now have a national system of inspection. And through OFSTED's monitoring and regulatory role, that reports are of a high quality.

When the inspection system was newly established there were some doubts as to whether it would work. These doubts are disappearing. Whilst any exercise of this scale is bound to have some teething problems there have been remarkably few complaints from schools about report findings. The use of Registered Inspectors has worked. Their status is high. There is now a healthy and competitive market in secondary school inspections and OFSTED have taken steps to ensure primary school inspections remain on target.

As an independent Government Department OFSTED can, rightly, focus on their core objective of ensuring the inspection of all schools. They are not beholden to LEAs but must answer to Parliament in discharging their statutory duty to 'secure that every school in England ... is inspected'.

For the longer term we will be watching to see the full impact of the inspection system. This will include the effect of HMCI's revised *Framework of Inspection*, due to be implemented during 1996. A number of interesting ideas are already been floated in the education world, for when the first cycle ends, including a suggestion that we adopt a longer inspection cycle for clearly satisfactory schools. We will consider these ideas carefully in the light of greater experience of the system. But whatever the final outcome any system must abide by the key principles: of independence, rigour, the rapid identification of schools that need help and the full publication of inspection reports.

Both Labour and Liberal Democrats opposed the Act which set up OFSTED throughout its passage through Parliament.

David Blunkett

Labour is developing policy on inspection and the way in which the Office for Standards in Education should develop and change. We believe that inspection should be a tool for improvement. It should ensure that comparative work takes place and encourage the spread of good practice. At present, the remit and operation of OFSTED achieves some but not all of our goals, while the way in which differing teaching methods are set against each other is not helpful.

Labour's paramount task is to improve standards, to increase achievement and to open opportunity to all our children, rather than simply a few. Mediocrity and failure cannot be tolerated, which is why a satisfactory inspection and advisory system is crucial. Restoring a balance and ensuring that the best of the past is brought forward to the future will be a key objective.

Her Majesty's Chief Inspector for Schools, Chris Woodhead, said in his 1993/94 report that 'significant numbers of primary and nursery schools were left without an inspection team'. His statement was backed up in a letter in December 1994 where he said that inspections for the Autumn Term had been 26 per cent below target in primary schools and 43 per cent below target in special and independent schools.

These facts served to illustrate some of the difficulties with the privatisation of inspection through Registered Inspectors (RgIs) which had emerged with the creation of the Office for Standards in Education. Essentially, the Government was finding it impossible to find sufficient freelance primary inspectors with the potential to cover the broad curricular range which characterises primary schools.

However, it would be wrong to suggest that there have not been some improvements. The greater frequency of inspections can only be welcomed, but targets set must be met if the credibility of the system is not to suffer further. Inspections have also become more evaluative, which offers teachers and parents a clearer idea of what might be done (although the Chief Inspector did find many inspectors' reports were below par in composition). There is however little help in implementing the recommendations.

Yet none of this is nearly enough. Britain still performs weakly in examination standards when compared with other major industrialised nations. The most recent OECD figures, from 1991, for the numbers of pupils obtaining a comparable upper secondary school qualification (equivalent to A-Levels/higher GNVQ) make sobering reading.

In Japan, 80 per cent achieve that standard. In Germany it is 68 per cent. In France – where they have an 80 per cent target for the Baccalaureate – it is 48 per cent. In England it is just 29 per cent. OECD figures for the numbers of 16 year olds reaching equivalent of GCSE grades A-C in maths, the national language and science for 1990/91 are of equal concern. There have been some improvements here since then, but the figures are still extremely worrying.

In France, 66 per cent gained their *premier cycle* exams. In Germany 62 per cent gained their *realschulabschluss*. In Japan 50 per cent of 15 year olds had reached that standard. But the English figure for GCSEs was just 27 per cent.

That is but one measure of the task facing the nation in raising standards. Inspection must be one of the tools used in assisting with that task. It is therefore not sufficient to criticise a school, nor indeed merely to suggest that standards can be improved, if the school cannot turn to external professionals for back-up and support.

There are clear weaknesses with the national system as it is constituted at present. There is, for example, inadequate training for new inspectors. The system relies very much on those from Her Majesty's Inspectorate and Local Education Authorities. When existing inspectors retire, there must be replacements ready or the backlog will expand. There are also weaknesses in the presentation of information to parents. Summary documents can distort the overall picture and a plainer English version of full reports might overcome concerns about such distortions.

However, the biggest weakness is the ambiguity in follow-up advice and support. There are probably two fairly key distinct, if complementary roles here: inspection and advice.

The independence of inspection is crucial. OFSTED must be independent, but responsible to ministers and Parliament. Its reports must be seen to be fair and honest. The development of any additional local inspections must be equally independent. There is considerable variation across the country, with Local Education Authorities providing in some cases excellent and complementary work, but others offering schools little of added value.

In the past, the Local Education Authority advisory services were hampered by a reputation in some areas in the country as the repository of those teachers who had failed in the classroom. While this reputation was deserved in some authorities, it was far from being universally the case. However, there are also legitimate concerns about the close relationship between some LEA inspectors and the schools being inspected. Independence of local inspection complemented by a highly professional and effective LEA advisory service should be the way forward.

Schools must feel confident that the inspection process is fair, rigorous and independent. Local management of schools has created a relationship based on partnership rather than 'interference' or 'domination' on the part of Local Education Authorities. A strong inspectorate must enhance that sense of working together.

Regular full inspection needs to be backed up by partial inspections and follow-ups to ensure that recommendations are being carried out. Schools can change considerably in character over a four-year period. So inspectors with a regional or local base should be able to monitor progress in the interim between regular national inspections. But while inspectors should be expected to answer questions from local education committees, they should be attached to the independent OFSTED network to ensure that their reports are clearly impartial. It would seem reasonable that local education committees and concerned school governors and parents should be able to ask inspectors to investigate where they feel there is cause for concern. The inspectorate could have the ability both to inspect individual departments of particular concern and to return more regularly to those departments exhibiting clear signs of difficulty, rather than having a full repeat OFSTED inspection. They could offer support and advice as appropriate.

The frequency of inspection must clearly be considered. Schools must have regular inspection. In the past, inspection was haphazard and infrequent – a situation which was clearly not acceptable. However, the frequency of inspection ought to relate to the potential problems faced by schools. Those in danger of failing must be inspected more often than schools where there is no reason to be concerned. The value of local or regional inspection should be to allow this to take place.

The Local Education Authority must be in a position to follow up the reports of inspectors. Schools should be able to request advice and support from the LEA to raise standards, improve management skills, enhance training or improve the curriculum. With delegation of budgets, the importance of these services being of a high standard is clear so that schools choose to buy quality support services from their LEA.

However, LEAs must be able to have one further role which should be used to tackle schools which are failing. Normally the aim will be to ensure that a failing school does not become a sink school. But *in extremis* it may be to remove the management team and governors from a failing school, to rename the school and introduce a new management team. We need to explore such ideas further, because the children's education and its continuity must be of paramount concern in this process.

The development of school appraisal should occur alongside an improvement in inspection. Schools which set targets in their Development Plans should include appraisal targets for teachers as a clear part of their plans for improvement.

But it is important that there is a consistency of quality in appraisal work. Linked to appraisal, there must be further training of head teachers and teachers to enhance their performance. For senior staff in particular, such retraining is crucial in ensuring that they are updated on developments and where they have such responsibilities that they develop their management skills.

It is equally important to recognise that where teachers or head teachers are consistently underperforming, they cannot expect to stay in front of a classroom or running a school. There must always be procedures which may well be beyond the appraisal system to ensure that this happens where such problems occur.

However, the primary role of appraisal must be to enhance and support the teacher in the classroom and the head teacher in running the school. A well-managed appraisal scheme should become a normal part of every teacher's professional life. Used well, it has a crucial role to play in the lifting of standards in all our schools.

Inspection has a crucial role to play in the drive to raise standards. As part of a process which is complemented by School Development Plans and teacher appraisal, a revived and reformed OFSTED can help to ensure that schools and pupils gain the maximum benefit from inspection.

Don Foster

Critics of current school inspection arrangements are fond of quoting the cliché that 'You don't fatten a pig by constantly weighing it'. But weighing does give some idea whether the pig needs fattening and, if so, by how much. So Liberal Democrats recognise that inspections of education at the point of delivery can provide a significant contribution to improving standards. However, under current arrangements, the potential is far from being realised.

Part of the failure stems from 'teething' rather than more fundamental problems. OFSTED is relatively new and some of the reported difficulties can and will be ironed out. For example, failure to recruit sufficient freelance inspectors has meant that many are working hours that have been compared with those of junior hospital doctors. And, acknowledging the need for improved inspector training, OFSTED itself has criticised as many as 1 in 8 inspection reports as being misleading, incomprehensible and inadequate.

It is also clear that current arrangements place undue, bureaucratic burdens on schools, especially small primary and nursery schools. Other concerns too, such as those relating to the need for increased confidentiality and anonymity of parents' communications with inspectors, the need for greater emphasis on home–school links and the need for increased time for consultation on a draft report, can and must be addressed. Nonetheless a recent, independent survey has indicated that only 25 per cent of inspected primary schools were dissatisfied with the work of their inspection team.

More fundamental problems do, however, exist. Many educationalists have welcomed, in principle, the establishment of a *Framework for Inspection* and the commitment to its review from time to time. But the assumption appears to be that if the criteria for successful schools can be specified clearly enough inspectors will be able to make judgements about them which are valid and reliable. The flaw in the argument is twofold. Firstly, a snapshot judgement against notional criteria makes no real allowance for local circumstances or the relevance of a school within the context of its local community needs. To ignore local baselines and contexts can only lead to demotivation of staff, often working against the odds in difficult circumstances. Secondly, the assumption ignores the nature of the judgements which, not least through time constraints, are partial, subjective and intuitive and, therefore, depend crucially on the experience of members of the inspection team.

Acknowledgement of these two limitations need only be a problem if the inspection system is seen, primarily, as a summative exercise. Liberal Democrats reject such a view which has led to Government actions severing the link between inspection and advice. Inspections should be treated as part of the formative process of school improvement and that requires the re-establishment of a link between inspection and advice. Such a move forms the basis of Liberal Democrat policy; a policy which sees OFSTED inspections as part of a continuous process and not discrete events.

Research on school effectiveness has illustrated that school improvement, although led by senior staff and governors, must involve and be the concern of everyone in the school. Developing quality must be a continuous process of review and development, individually planned in each school. External inspections by OFSTED must link into that process. Building on current practice, Liberal Democrats would require each school to produce an Institutional Development Plan (IDP) designed to cover at least a three-year period. The IDP would be expected to integrate the school's budgetary strategy with plans to rectify areas of weakness identified in any earlier OFSTED inspection and details of the priorities for the school's self-review. Subsequent inspections would, in addition to a consideration of the notional criteria in the *Framework for Inspection*, provide external moderation of the school's own review process.

LEAs too should have a greater role in the process. There is little point in an inspection system which identifies problems in a particular school when there is no help and advice available to help the school overcome the problems. Recent Government cuts in local authority budgets have meant that the advisory services in many LEAs have been reduced. Remaining advisors are often so busy tendering for, and conducting, OFSTED inspections that they have little time to help their own, local schools.

Liberal Democrats would strengthen LEA advisory teams and redefine their role in the school improvement process to enable them to share in the moderation of each school's review process, to ensure that each school is using its GEST funding to 'purchase' appropriate external advice and support and, when requested by a school, to provide such support.

Within such a process there is less need for a regular four-yearly cycle of OFSTED inspections. The cycle could be lengthened, perhaps to six or seven years, with greater use, as appropriate, of the existing procedures whereby various bodies from Secretary of State to school governors can initiate an inspection. Thus, for example, an LEA advisory service unhappy with the decisions and actions of a school has the 'sanction' of calling for a further OFSTED inspection.

Notwithstanding the significant role of inspections in the formative process of school improvement, independent, external inspections also have a summative role; the collective results of individual inspections can provide information about the state of the education service needed to determine future policy. To enhance this role and to ensure nationally consistent standards, Liberal Democrats would significantly increase the number of HMIs who would, among other duties (including the monitoring of LEA advisory services), perform the functions of Registered Inspectors. Their teams would, as at present, be made up of OFSTED trained personnel but, additionally, OFSTED would be given powers to approve or otherwise, the composition of an inspection team. OFSTED would determine which schools were to be inspected and when, and draw up a contract for the inspection with the relevant HMI. The bidding process would end and inspectors would be paid on a nationally agreed scale. OFSTED itself would be accountable directly to Parliament for its managerial functions but it and HMI would remain independent in respect of their judgements about educational provision.

Liberal Democrats have quality at the centre of the entire range of their education policies. These proposals would take a major step towards ensuring that standards in schools improve by not only weighing the pig, but also by encouraging it to alter its diet in such a way that it fattens in all the right places.

Concluding Note

The contributors to this book have offered many different perspectives on the inspection process. Several common themes emerge. One of these is the extent to which the OFSTED process is leading schools into a common pattern of practice and reducing diversity. Several contributors to this volume (and Hargreaves 1995) argue that this may be so. Research is clearly needed on the impact of an impending inspection on a school. While our research findings suggest that the preparation for inspection was not *perceived* as having a more powerful influence on school practice than the inspection itself, informal evidence suggests that schools do make many changes in the way they work in the months before an inspection. This issue needs further research.

Our own recent research has, however, surprised us by how positive most schools are about inspection. Most of those we followed up two years after their inspection have positive things to say about its outcomes. They do not appear to report being pushed into doing things they didn't want to do. Rather they seem to welcome the fact that the inspectors tell them things that they half knew already. This gives them the impetus to 'get going'. It may also give them permission to take on issues that have been put to one side over the years. But they do seem to feel that the direction they take is theirs, rather than the inspectors.

It is clear that outside consultancy can be very helpful to schools developing their practice. It has often been pointed out that a weakness of the OFSTED process is that the inspectors leave when the report is presented and do not help with implementing change. But if the OFSTED inspectors did continue to work with the school in a consultancy role the anxieties of those who fear a single OFSTED-model school all over the country might be even more justified. It might be better for schools to choose their own consultants (possibly a member of their inspection team) who fit with their educational values rather than being required to use the OFSTED team.

In our research the small group who are extremely critical are, as Hargreaves (1995) suggests they might be, the very traditional (often selective) schools which are popular with parents but felt to be not achieving their potential by inspectors. In these cases there is a tension between the values of the customers (the parents), and the values of the regulators (the inspectors). In the education market place, which should have the most influence over schools?

OFSTED published its first major revision of the *Handbook* in November 1995. They claim that this will be less burdensome for both schools and inspectors, and take more account of particular features of the individual school. There have already been questions raised about the validity and reliability of the inspection process. Do inspectors make similar judgements to each other when faced with similar evidence? Can the process ever be as 'objective' as OFSTED claims? Should it try to be? Will the revisions make the process even less comparable across schools? This again raises the question of what OFSTED inspections are for. Are they for improvement or for accountability? Should they be (in Maw's terms) 'high stakes' or 'low stakes'?

A way forward in combining these two needs might be by changing the focus from inspecting schools to inspecting the 'quality assurance systems' of schools (Hargreaves 1995). The schools themselves would be required to provide OFSTED with information which would also be useful for their own development, but this would require a radical change in the use of inspectors' time. At present 70 per cent of an inspection is spent in classrooms. If it focused more on quality assurance systems then the classroom would become a less important part of the whole inspection process. But the process would have to remain close to the classroom in spirit or it might become yet another exercise to be gone through which had little relevance to the daily work of teachers and pupils.

Training of inspectors is clearly an issue for the future. If the inspection process is either by design or by implication 'high stakes' then inspectors must be fully trained to provide the quality of data that a 'high stakes' system requires. All inspectors will need regular updating and refreshing so that their judgements and interpretations are valid. At present Registered Inspectors, and team members themselves are responsible for team members' in-service training. This will be particularly important as the new *Handbook* is implemented in mid-1996.

At present inspection is an under-researched area. Some of the studies have been undertaken by OFSTED (e.g. 1994f, 1995d) but there is currently little independent work beyond that included in this book and in the *Cambridge Journal of Education* (Volume 25, Number 1, March 1995). OFSTED's own studies are understandably within their own conceptual framework. They tend to ask *how* the inspection system is working, not *whether* it should be working as it is. Research by 'outsiders' is clearly needed: inspection has become a high profile and expensive part of national education provision, and the education community generally should have access to research to inform its decision-making.

References

Airasian, P.W. (1988) 'Symbolic validation: the case of state-mandated, high-stakes testing', *Educational Evaluation and Policy Analysis*, **10**(4).

Alexander, R., Rose, J. and Woodhead, C. (1992) *Curriculum Organisation and Classroom Practice in Primary Schools – a discussion paper* (The 'Three Wise Men' Report). London: DES.

Audit Commission (1984) *Code of Local Government Audit Practice for England and Wales*. London: HMSO.

Baker, K. (1988) Speech to CLEA, January.

Ball, S. (1990a) *Politics and Policy Making in Education: Explorations in Policy Sociology*. London: Routledge.

Ball, S. (1990b) *Foucault and Education: Disciplines and Knowledge*. London: Routledge.

Ball, S. (1993) 'Education policy, power relations, and teachers' work', *British Journal of Educational Studies*, **XXXI**(?.).

Bernstein, B. (1990) *Structuring of Pedagogic Discourse Class, Codes and Social Control*, Volume 4. London: Routledge.

Bernstein, B. (1993) Santiago Conference Address (Unpublished paper, Institute of Education, London.)

Blackburne, L. (1994) 'Inspectorship course under fire', *Times Educational Supplement*, 14 October.

Bolton, E. (1991) 'A view from the top', *Times Educational Supplement*, 21 June.

Bolton, E. (1993) 'Alternative education policies: school inspection'. IPPR Goldsmith Seminar, Institute of Education, University of London. (Unpublished.)

Bowring-Carr, G. (1995) Letter, *Times Educational Supplement*, 17 February.

Brimblecombe, N., Ormston, M. and Shaw, M. (1995) 'Teachers' perceptions of school inspection: a stressful experience', *Cambridge Journal of Education*, **25**(1).

Budge, D. (1994) 'Time steals a march on lay army', *Times Educational Supplement*, 10 June.

Burchill, J. (1991) *Inspecting Schools: Breaking the Monopoly*. London: Centre for Policy Studies.

Churcher, J. (1994) 'A primary school inspector is born', *Management in Education*, **8**(4), 8.

Clarke, K. (1991) 'Power to the people's HMI', *Times Educational Supplement*, 1 November.

Clarke, L. (1976) *The Inspector Remembers*. London: Dennis Dobson.

Committee of the Privy Council for Education (1840) *Instructions to Inspectors*. Minutes.

Coopers & Lybrand/OFSTED (1994) *A Focus on Quality*. London: HMSO.

Cunningham, P. (1988) *Curriculum Change in the Primary School since 1945*. Basingstoke: Falmer Press.

Davies, B. (1994) 'On the neglect of pedagogy in educational studies and its consequences', *British Journal of In-service Education*, **20**(1), 17–34.

Dean, J. (1994) *What Headteachers and Teachers Think About Inspection*. NFER, Slough: EMIE

Department for Education (DFE) (1992a) *Choice and Diversity: A New Framework for Schools*. London: HMSO.

Department for Education (DFE) (1992b) Education (Schools) Act 1992. London: HMSO.

Department for Education (DFE) (1992c) *Inspecting schools: A guide to the inspection provision of the Education (Schools) Act 1992*. London: DFE.

Department for Education (DFE) (1993) Circular 7/93. London: HMSO.

Department of Education and Science (DES) (1978) *Primary Education in England: A Survey by HMI*. London: HMSO.

Department of Education and Science (DES) (1979) *Aspects of Secondary Education in England: A Survey by HMI*. London: HMSO.

Department of Education and Science (DES) (1982) *Study of HM Inspectorate in England and Wales* (The Rayner Report). London: HMSO.

Department of Education and Science (DES) (1984) *Initial Teacher Training: Approval of Courses*. London: HMSO.

Department of Education and Science (DES) (1988) *Education Reform Act: Local Management of Schools*. London: DES.

Department of Education and Science (DES) (1989a) *Planning for School Development: Advice to Governors, Headteachers and Teachers, Circular 24/89*. London: DES.

Department of Education and Science (DES) (1989b) *Standards in Education: Annual Report of HM Senior Inspector*. London: HMSO.

Department of Education and Science (DES) (1989c) *Initial Teacher Training: Approval of Courses*. London: HMSO.

Department of Education and Science (DES) (1990) *Standards in Education: Annual Report of HM Senior Inspector*. London: HMSO.

Department of Education and Science (DES) (1991a) *Development Planning: A Practical Guide*. London: DES.

Department of Education and Science (DES) (1991b) *Standards in Education: Annual Report of HM Senior Inspector*. London: HMSO.

Department of Education and Science (DES) (1991c) *HMI in the 1990s: The Work of HM Inspectors*. London: HMSO.

Earley, P., Fidler, B. and Ouston, J. (eds) (1996) *Improvement Through Inspection? Complementary Approaches to School Development*. London: David Fulton Publishers.

Fairclough, N. (1992) *Discourse and Social Change*. Cambridge: Polity Press.

Fidler, B., Bowles, G. and Hart, J. (1991) *Effective Local Management of Schools Workbook: Planning Your School's Strategy*. London: Longman.

Fish, S. (1980) *Is There a Text in This Class? The Authority of Interpretive Communities*. Cambridge, Mass.: Harvard University Press.

Fish, S. (1989) *Doing what comes naturally: change, rhetoric and the practice of theory in literary and legal studies*. Oxford: Oxford University Press.

Fish, S. (1994) *There's No Such Thing as Free Speech, and it's a Good Thing, Too*. New York: Oxford University Press.

171
Foucault, M. (1979) *Discipline and Punish: the Birth of the Prison*. London: Allan Lane.

Fullan, M. (1991) *The New Meaning of Educational Change*. London: Cassell.

Fullan, M. (1992) *What's Worth Fighting for in Headship?* Milton Keynes: Open University Press.

Further Education Funding Council (FEFC) (1993) *Assessing Achievement*, Circular 93/28. London: FEFC.

Gipps, C.V. (1994) *Beyond Testing*. Lewes: Falmer Press.

Glynn, J. (1987) *Public Sector Financial Control and Accounting*. Oxford: Blackwell.

Gray, J. and Wilcox, B. (1994) 'In the aftermath of inspection: the nature and fate of inspection report recommendations'. Presentation to the BERA Conference. Oxford University. September.

Hackett, G. (1994) 'Inspection backlog fear', *Times Educational Supplement*, 9 July.

Hargreaves, A. (1994) *Changing Teachers, Changing Times: Teachers' Work and Culture in the Postmodern Age*. London: Cassell.

Hargreaves, D. (1990) 'Making schools more effective: the challenge to policy, practice and research', *Scottish Education Review*, (22), 1.

Hargreaves, D. (1993) *The Mosaic of Learning*. London: DEMOS.

Hargreaves, D. (1995) 'Inspection and school improvement', *Cambridge Journal of Education*, **25**(1), 117–25.

Hargreaves, D. and Hopkins, D. (1991) *The Empowered School*. London: Cassell.

Hargreaves, D., Hopkins, D., Leask, M., Connolly, J. and Robinson, P. (1989) *Planning for School Development*. London: DES.

Hillgate Group (1986) *Whose Schools? A Radical Manifesto*. London: Hillgate Group.

Hillgate Group (1987) *The Reform of British Education: from Principles to Practice*. London: Hillgate Group.

HMI (1990) *HMI in the Nineties*. London: DFE.

HMI (1993) *Aspects of School Review in South Australia*. London: HMSO.

Hopes, C. (1991) *School Inspectorates in the Member States of the European Community*. Frankfurt am Main: Deutshes Institut für Internationale Pädagogische Forschung.

Hopkins, D., Ainscow, M. and West, M. (1994) *School Improvement in an Era of Change*. London: Cassell.

Hoskin, K. (1990) 'Foucault under examination: the crypto-educationalist unmasked' in Ball, S. (ed.) *Foucault and Education: Disciplines and Knowledge*. London: Routledge.

Hustler, D., Goodwin, A. and Roden, M. (1995) 'Early days for Lay Inspectors', *Research in Education* (forthcoming)

Joyce, B. (1991) 'The doors to school improvement', *Educational Leadership*, **48**(8).

Kyriacou, C. (1990) 'The nature and sources of stress facing teachers', *Education Section Review*, **14**(2), 37–40.

Lee, J. and Fitz, J. (1994) 'Inspecting for improvement: HMI and curriculum development in England and Wales'. Paper presented to AERA Annual Meeting, New Orleans, April. (Unpublished.)

Levačić, R. and Glover, D. (1994) *OFSTED Assessment of Schools' Efficiency: an analysis of 66 secondary school inspection reports*. Milton Keynes: Open University.

172

The LMS Initiative (1988) *Local Management in Schools: A Practical Guide.* London: The LMS Initiative.

MacGilchrist, B. and Savage, J. (1994) 'The Impact of School Development Planning in Primary Schools: Early Findings'. Paper presented to BERA Conference. Oxford University.

Madaus, G. (1988) 'The influence of testing on the curriculum' in Tanner (ed.) *Critical Issues in Curriculum 87th Yearbook of NSSE.* Chicago: University of Chicago Press.

Maw, J. (1994) *Calling HMI to Account.* London: Tufnell Press.

Maw, J. (1995) 'The Handbook for the Inspection of Schools: a critique', *Cambridge Journal of Education,* 25(1).

McMahon, A. et al. (1984) *Guidelines for Review and Internal Development in Schools (GRIDS).* London: Longman.

Metcalfe, C. (1994) 'Inspection and quality: the contribution of research'. Presentation to the BERA Conference, September.

Millet, A. (1993) 'How inspectors can actually help', *Times Educational Supplement,* 25 June.

Northam, J.A. (1993) OFSTED's First Hundred. Walpole House Occasional Papers No. 1. London: St Mary's University College.

Northam, J.A. (1994a) OFSTED Reports on Primary & Nursery Schools. Walpole House Occasional Papers No. 2. London: St Mary's University College.

Northam, J.A. (July 1994b) OFSTED Reports on Secondary Schools. Walpole House Occasional Papers No. 3. London: St Mary's University College.

O'Connor, M. (1995) 'Revelations after the storm', *Times Educational Supplement,* 20 January.

Office for Standards in Education (OFSTED) (1993a) *Corporate Plan 1993–94 to 1995–96.* London: OFSTED.

Office for Standards in Education (OFSTED) (1993b) *Aspects of School Review in South Australia.* London: HMSO.

Office for Standards in Education (OFSTED) (1993c) *Handbook for the Inspection of Schools.* London: HMSO.

Office for Standards in Education (OFSTED) (1993d) *Framework for the Inspection of Schools.* London: OFSTED.

Office for Standards in Education (OFSTED) (1993e) *Guidance on the Inspection Schedule.* London: OFSTED.

Office for Standards in Education (OFSTED) (1994a) *Handbook for the Inspection of Schools* (Consolidated Edition). London: HMSO.

Office for Standards in Education (OFSTED) (1994b) *Framework for the Inspection of Schools.* London: OFSTED.

Office for Standards in Education (OFSTED) (1994c) *Assessing School Effectiveness.* London: HMSO.

Office for Standards in Education (OFSTED) (1994d) *Primary Matters: A Discussion of Teaching and Learning in Primary Schools.* London: HMSO.

Office for Standards in Education (OFSTED) (1994e) *Independent Inspections of Secondary Schools, 1993–4.* London: OFSTED.

Office for Standards in Education (OFSTED) (1994f) *A Focus on Quality.* London: HMSO.

Office for Standards in Education (OFSTED) (1994g) *Improving Schools.* London: HMSO.

Office for Standards in Education (OFSTED) (1994h) *Guidance on the Inspection Schedule.* London: OFSTED.

Office for Standards in Education (OFSTED) (1995a) *The Annual Report of Her Majesty's Chief Inspector of Schools 1993/4*. London: HMSO.

Office for Standards in Education (OFSTED) (1995b) *New Framework for the Inspection of Schools: Draft for Consultation*. London: HMSO.

Office for Standards in Education (OFSTED) (1995c) *Mathematics: A Review of Inspection Findings*. London: HMSO.

Office for Standards in Education (OFSTED) (1995d) *Inspection Quality 1994–5*. London: OFSTED.

Ormston, M. and Shaw, M. (1993) *Inspection: a preparation guide for schools*. London: Longman.

Ouston, J. and Klenowski, V. (1995) *The OFSTED Experience: The Parents' Eye View*. London: Research and Information on State Education Trust (RISE).

Ouston, J., Fidler, B. and Earley, P. (1995) 'School improvement through school inspection?' American Educational Research Association Conference 1995 (and Chapter 11 in this book).

Punch, K. and Tuettemann, E. (1990) 'Correlates of psychological distress among secondary school teachers', *British Educational Research Journal*, 16(4), 369-81.

Pyke, N. (1995) 'TTA's first target is poor recruits', *Times Educational Supplement*, 16 June.

RISE (1994) *The OFSTED Experience: a Governor's Eye View*. London: Research and Information on State Education Trust (RISE).

Rose, J. (1995) 'Subject to scrutiny, *Times Educational Supplement*, 10 March.

Rudduck, J. (1991) *Innovation and Change*. Milton Keynes: Open University Press.

Samph, T. (1976) 'Observer effects in teacher verbal behaviour' *Journal of Educational Psychology*, 68(6), 736-41.

Shaw, M., Brimblecombe, N. and Ormston, M. (1995) 'It ain't what you do, it's the way that you do it', *Management in Education*, 9(1).

Simon, B. (1985) *Does Education Matter?* London: Lawrence and Wishart.

Tytler, D. (1993) 'School inspectors: butchers miss the Lay inspections', *Guardian*, 7 September.

White, C. (1995) 'Avoid excesses of traditionalists and progressives', *Times Higher Education Supplement*, 10 February.

Wilcox, B. (1992) *Time Constrained Evaluation*. London: Routledge.

Wilcox, B. and Gray, J. (1994) 'Reactions to inspection', *Cambridge Journal of Education*, 24(2), 245–59.

Wilcox, B. and Gray, J. (1995) 'The OFSTED inspection model: the views of LEA chief inspectors', *Cambridge Journal of Education*, 25(1), 63–73.

Woodhead, C. (1995) 'Education: the elusive engagement and continuing frustration'. Annual Lecture, Royal Society of Arts, 28 January.

Wragg, T. (1987) *Teacher Appraisal: a Practical Guide*. London: Macmillan Education.

Wragg, T. (1995) 'A parallel universe in paper, my dears', *Times Educational Supplement*, 6 January.

Index